7
SEVEN
BLESSINGS
OF THE
ATONEMENT

7 SEVEN BLESSINGS OF THE ATONEMENT

UNLEASH THE ANCIENT DOUBLE-PORTION PROMISES IN YOUR LIFE TODAY

STEVE MUNSEY

CLARION CALL MARKETING

DALLAS, TEXAS

PART 3: GREATER THINGS

7 SEVEN BLESSINGS OF THE ATONEMENT

UNLEASH THE ANCIENT
DOUBLE-PORTION PROMISES
IN YOUR LIFE TODAY

STEVE MUNSEY

CLARION CALL MARKETING

DALLAS, TEXAS

SEVEN BLESSINGS OF THE ATONEMENT

Published by Clarion Call Marketing
P.O. Box 610010
Dallas, TX 75261

© 2006 Clarion Call Marketing

All Scripture quotations, unless otherwise indicated, are taken from the *New King James Version*. Copyright © 1982 by Thomas Nelson, Inc. Used by permission. All rights reserved.

Scripture quotations marked (KJV) are taken from the *King James Version*.

Scripture quotations marked (NIV) are taken from the *Holy Bible, New International Version*, NIV®. Copyright © 1973, 1978, 1984 by International Bible Society. Used by permission of Zondervan Publishing House. All rights reserved.

ISBN 1-59574-965-1

Printed in the United States of America

2006—First Edition

10 9 8 7 6 5 4 3 2

CONTENTS

PART 3: GREATER THINGS

INTRODUCTION

And the LORD spoke to Moses, saying, "Speak to the children of Israel, and say to them: 'The feasts of the LORD, which you shall proclaim to be holy convocations, these are My feasts.'... Also the tenth day of this seventh month shall be the Day of Atonement. It shall be a holy convocation for you; you shall afflict your souls, and offer an offering made by fire to the LORD."

—LEVITICUS 23:1-2, 27

In Leviticus, God instructed Moses to observe the "feasts of the Lord," but what does an ancient Hebrew commemoration called the Day of Atonement have to do with Christian believers nearly 3,500 years after the day of fasting and prayer began to be observed?

What started out as a time of personal Bible study for me has now spanned the globe and spawned two books. No one could be more surprised than I am!

Several years ago, the Lord began directing me to study intently on the subject of the seven feasts which were given to Moses and the children of Israel, as found in Leviticus 23 and throughout the Bible.

I ended up sharing what the Lord impressed upon my heart with the precious people who attended the church I have pastored for many years, Family Christian Center, in Munster, Indiana. The response was simply amazing to me, for I knew it was very interesting on a personal level, yet I was pleasantly surprised to see others "getting it," too, and beginning to discover for themselves what God had in store for them.

Since that time, God has given me the opportunity to minister from some of the nation's best pulpits and the largest Christian television networks. I began speaking on the Leviticus 23 feasts to these audiences, and the results continued to spread.

As a result, eventually God directed me to write a book with the specific title, *Seven Blessings of the Passover.* That book has since circled the globe in different languages. Over and over, I receive reports from people who have heard me teach about this subject on television or have read my book, and then they decided to accept the challenge of observing the Passover and giving a special offering, and their lives have changed forever as blessing upon blessing has been heaped upon them. Again, I am more amazed than anyone how widespread this has become!

Of course, I know that others have been receiving this revelation from the Lord, but I feel as if my little personal Bible study has been used of God to touch a lot of lives. To Him be all the glory!

I say all that to point to the fact that I am now feeling the same compulsion and direction to write this book, focusing on the Day of Atonement and its seven very specific blessings.

THE FEASTS

From the beginning, as with most Christians today, I approached the study of the seven feasts mentioned in Leviticus 23 with a "take it or leave it" attitude. My personal journey took a different turn when I discovered the meaning of the two Hebrew words found in that chapter: *mo'ed* (verse 2) and *chag* (verse 6). Both are translated "feasts" in English, but they have even more meaning when you seek to understand the true Hebrew meaning:

- In verse 2, the word for feast is the Hebrew word *mo'ed*, as it is written, *"Speak to the children of Israel, and say to them: 'The feasts of the LORD, which you shall proclaim to be holy convocations, these are My feasts.'"* The word *mo'ed* means "an appointment, a fixed time or season, a cycle or year, an assembly, an appointed time, a set time, or exact time." [1] By instructing with the word *mo'ed*, God set an appointment with His followers for a specific reason.

- In verse 6, the word *chag* is used: *"And on the fifteenth day of the same month is the Feast of Unleavened Bread to the LORD."* The English word closest to the meaning of this word is "festival." [2] According to Strong's *Exhaustive Concordance*, *chag* is taken from the Hebrew word *chagag*, defined as "to move in a circle, to march in a sacred procession, to celebrate, dance, to hold a solemn feast or holiday." [3] God clearly gave these cyclical festivals to be observed year after year.

Why were these seven feasts or festivals started? More importantly, what did God want to teach His children through the specific instructions He gave as He instituted these appointed times?

Before we can answer that question, it is important to have a brief history lesson, as I did in my Passover book: [4]

- As part of the Exodus from Egypt, as recorded in Exodus 12, God instituted seven feasts. In Leviticus 23, God additionally instructed the children of Israel to hold seven holy gatherings each year, celebrated during three feast seasons.

- God designed seven feasts for the Israelites (Leviticus 23). These feasts were God's own Holy Days, and there were specific instructions given for their observance. God Himself orchestrated the sequence and time of each of these feasts.

- The feasts fall into three clusters: the Passover season (the Feasts of Passover, Unleavened Bread, and Firstfruits), the Feast of Weeks (also known as Pentecost), and the Tabernacles season (Trumpets, Atonement, and Tabernacles).

- During these times the Israelites were to appear together before the Lord. The Word of God strictly instructed them that they must not appear before Him without an offering. Deuteronomy 16:16) states: *"And they shall not appear before the LORD empty-handed."*

- The last three gatherings, the Feast of Trumpets, Day of Atonement, and Feast of Tabernacles, extend over a period of twenty-one days in the fall of the year. They are known collectively as "Tabernacles."

Each of these feasts was extremely significant for Israel, and they honored God for what He had done. Every feast points us to the Son of God and very special blessings assigned to each time of appointment.

THREE SEASONS—SEVEN FEASTS

All of these feasts were extremely significant times for the Hebrews, for they taught the children of Israel and their descendents to honor God for what He had done in their lives. More importantly, each feast pointed to the Messiah, distinctively describing a vital part of His life and ministry:

Passover Season

The first three feasts—Passover, Unleavened Bread, and Firstfruits— occur during the spring of the year over a period of eight days. Referred to collectively as "Passover," its purpose was (and is) to teach the children of Israel how to find and enter God's true rest.

The Bible commanded that the various feasts of the Passover season were to be kept in their appointed seasons: *"Let the children of Israel also keep the passover at his appointed season. In the fourteenth day of this month, at even, ye shall keep it in his appointed season:*

according to all the rites of it, and according to all the ceremonies thereof, *shall ye keep it"* (Numbers 9:2-3, KJV).

During the Feast of the Passover (Leviticus 23:4-5), the Lamb died so we might receive salvation. In the Feast of Unleavened Bread (23:6-8), we received deliverance from sin, so we must turn from our disobedience. In the Feast of Firstfruits (23:9-14), we rise with new life, a new creation, leaving the old things behind.

Pentecost Season

The fourth feast, Feast of Weeks, also known as Pentecost, occurs fifty days (the Greek name *Pentecost* means "fifty") later at the beginning of the summer. It was a single gathering (Leviticus 23:15-22). During this feast the Hebrews were taught specifically how to receive and live in God's supernatural power.

Tabernacles Season

The third season of feasts is collectively known as Tabernacles. This season included the Feast of Trumpets, Day of Atonement, and Feast of Tabernacles. Always the most glorious season of all and celebrated over twenty-one days in the fall of each year, the purpose of this season was to teach the children of Israel how to enter God's protection.

In the Feast of Trumpets (Leviticus 23:23-25), the gathering of Israel points to repentance and incorruption of the saints of God. During the Feast of Atonement (23:26-32), prayer, righteousness, and faith are emphasized through supernatural cleansing. And during the Feast of Tabernacles (23:33-44), the main themes are fruit, harvest, and latter rain, pointing to the ultimate reign of the Messiah.

I will focus more specifically on the Tabernacles season in chapter 2. Suffice it to say that each of these seven feasts presented (and still do) an opportunity for the children of Israel and their descendents to honor God for what He had done in their lives. These were God's own holy days, and specific instructions were given for their observance.

Through ancient times, the children of Israel traveled to Jerusalem three times a year to commemorate these feasts. As a special note, it is important to realize that the Jewish calendar is based on the lunar cycle, so it is different from our Gregorian or Julian calendar, both based on the solar cycles. The Jewish calendar is eleven days shorter than a solar-based calendar. To reconcile the difference between our solar-based calendar (365.25 days) and the lunar year (354 days), the Jewish calendar is based upon a nineteen-year cycle in which the third, sixth, eighth, eleventh, fourteenth, seventeenth, and nineteenth years are leap years. It is for this reason that the feasts do not fall on the same day each year of the calendars we use today.

WHY NOT TODAY?

While Jewish people around the world continue to observe the seven feasts, the observance fell into disuse among Christians after AD 325. That was the year the Roman Emperor Flavius Valerius Constantinus convened the Council of Nicaea. Known better as Constantine the Great, he converted to Christianity—a wonderful thing—then decided to unite the many Christian groups throughout his kingdom. Many changes (some not so wonderful as Constantine's conversion!) happened as a result of the Nicene Council, including:

- The date of observance of Jesus's birth became December 25.

- The day of worship was moved from the Sabbath (Saturday) to the first day of each week (Sunday).

- The doctrine of the Trinity was confirmed as orthodox Christian belief.

- The Church of Rome was officially established.

One of the important teachings omitted from Constantine's Creed—as a result of the Nicene Council—was the observance of the "Hebrew" feasts. Some believe that Constantine had seen that God's people were blessed as a result of observing the feasts, and as a consequence, perhaps to keep them from getting too much power—financially, spiritually, or politically—he stopped their adherence to God's command of observing the feasts.

Regardless of his reasons, since AD 325, celebrating the holy convocations (the feasts) has largely not been a part of the church knowledge or practice. It is time to change that perception. It is time to move into the blessings that God provided to those who observe the feasts!

Why Study These Seven Feasts?

I wish I had a dollar for every time I've been asked why we should study these feasts? I run into people all the time whose eyes glaze over at the mere mention of anything dealing with the Old Testament. They say, "I don't get it. What's with the symbolism and 'begats' and the ancient ceremonies? What do those things have to do with the New Testament and how believers should live today?"

Others bring out the well-worn statement, "We're not under the law anymore. We're under grace. All of those Hebrew laws passed away after the cross."

As recorded in Matthew 5:17, the Savior told His followers very clearly, *"Do not think that I came to destroy the Law or the Prophets. I did not come to destroy but to fulfill."*

Granted (and thanks be to God!), we *are* redeemed by the blood of Jesus Christ. We don't have to follow the ancient blood sacrifices for our sins to be atoned. That *was* settled at the cross. However, what God gave to us in the Old Testament is extremely important to know and understand in order to become what God expects us to be today.

In fact, it is impossible to truly understand what God gave us in the New Testament unless we grasp and build on the foundation of the Old Testament. Benny Hinn says this best:

> All the foundations for the final twenty-seven books of the Bible are laid in the first thirty-nine books. The New Testament is the fulfillment of the Old. Each is incomplete without the other.
>
> The New in the Old is concealed; the Old in the New is revealed! Praise God for the fact that we have both.
>
> And one of the most remarkable treasures in all of

Scripture is the study of the feasts which God outlined through the instructions He gave to the children of Israel. [5]

The feasts of Israel were built upon the foundation of God's blood covenant with mankind. This goes back to Adam and Eve, who lived in a perfect world, blameless, and without guilt. The first man and woman knew God intimately. They walked with Him and fellowshipped with Him regularly. Then they rebelled through a sin of disobedience. They ate from the Tree of Knowledge of Good and Evil. This is more than a mere allegory. It is the basis for all that follows for mankind, as presented throughout both the Old and New Testaments.

Again, let me quote Benny Hinn: "The feasts of Israel…are graphic object lessons. From the time they were given to the children of Israel, these laws were ever-present visual aids, or pictures, if you will, to use physical rituals to help them understand spiritual truth and to walk therein." [6]

SEVEN BLESSINGS OF THE ATONEMENT

Of all the seven yearly appointments with God, the Day of Atonement was (and still is) the most solemn and awe-filled of commemorations. It was a time set aside for national and sanctuary cleansing. On this day special sacrifices were offered for atonement or reconciliation.

God established the Day of Atonement to be kept forever: *"So this day shall be to you a memorial; and you shall keep it as a feast to the* LORD *throughout your generations. You shall keep it as a feast by an everlasting ordinance"* (Exodus 12:14). This feast was established not only for the Israelites in the time of their flight from Egypt, but also consecrated as an "appointed [holy] time" each year throughout both the Old and the New Testaments. I will detail more about this in chapters 1 and 2.

Lost through the centuries since AD 325 is the fact that God promised blessings to those who observe His feasts. Specifically, those obedient in the Day of Atonement were promised seven blessings—seven specific, supernatural atonement blessings:

1. A double portion on the economy

2. Financial blessings

3. Restoration

4. Special miracles

5. A divine presence

6. Blessings upon your family

7. Deliverance

However, for nearly seventeen centuries, these powerful truths have been mostly ignored and even rejected by Christians. Thankfully, that is now changing. It must change! There is too much at stake during these crucial, prophetic days.

As I said, God has been stirring me to write this book for years since I started my own personal study. I believe the time is perfect now to tell people how their lives will change dramatically when they restore the Day of Atonement observance and offering, for God absolutely, positively sets schedules and time boundaries, especially for His feasts and blessings.

I also know, based upon my own life and the testimonies of people all around the globe, that God is poised to pour out these seven blessings upon your life. As you read *Seven Blessings of the Atonement*, you can unleash these very special ancient blessings in your life today.

It is my prayer that God will use the pages of this book to revolutionize your life and that He will pour out more blessings than you ever dreamed possible. More than anything, I pray that you will understand why God wants you to receive these seven blessings. I know your life will be changed forever as a result!

—Steve Munsey

PART ONE

ATONEMENT

1

THE DAY
OF ATONEMENT

And the LORD spoke to Moses, saying, "Speak to the children of Israel, and say to them: 'The feasts of the LORD, which you shall proclaim to be holy convocations, these are My feasts.... These are the feasts of the LORD, holy convocations which you shall proclaim at their appointed times."

—LEVITICUS 23:1-2, 4

After the Exodus—the great escape and deliverance from captivity in Egypt—the children of Israel were instructed by God to hold seven holy gatherings each year and established them on the Jewish calendar.

The feasts fall into three groups—the Passover season (the Feasts of Passover, Unleavened Bread, and Firstfruits), the Feast of Weeks (also known as Pentecost), and the Tabernacles season (Trumpets, Atonement, and Tabernacles). These represented the three major links between God and His covenant children. These feasts also related directly to Israel's agricultural seasons.

Since this book deals primarily with the blessings of the sixth convocation, let me focus on the third season which occurs during the fall of each year. Tabernacles includes three special holy times— the Feast of Trumpets, the Day of Atonement, and the Feast of Tabernacles. Each is closely related, and to understand the seven blessings of the atonement, it is vital to understand the basics of each feast.

THE FEAST OF TRUMPETS

Also called the High Holy Days or Rosh Hashanah, Trumpets is the first of the fall feasts. *Rosh Hashanah*, which means "head of year," signals the start of the civil year and is observed in the autumn of the year. On the Hebrew calendar, it occurs on the first day of Tishri, the seventh Hebrew month—mid September to early October, annually. The civil new year was decided in the second century AD, right after the destruction of the Temple and more than 1,500 years after its inception in the time of Moses. All of this is on the Jewish calendar. Note that it is important to remember that we live by the Gregorian calendar, while the Jews and the Bible are set on the Hebrew calendar.

Ezra the scribe related that it was during the Feast of Trumpets that the temple altar was rebuilt and sacrificial offerings were reinstituted by those who returned from Babylonian exile:

And when the seventh month had come, and the children of Israel were in the cities, the people gathered together as one man to Jerusalem. Then Jeshua the son of Jozadak and his brethren the priests, and Zerubbabel the son of Shealtiel and his brethren, arose and built the altar of the God of Israel, to offer burnt offerings on it, as it is written in the Law of Moses the man of God. Though fear had come upon them because of the people of those countries, they set the altar on its bases; and they offered burnt offerings on it to the LORD, both the morning and evening burnt offerings. They also kept the Feast of Tabernacles, as it is written, and offered the daily burnt offerings in the number required by ordinance for each day. Afterwards they offered the regular burnt offering, and those for New Moons and for all the appointed feasts of the LORD that were consecrated, and those of everyone who willingly offered a freewill offering to the LORD. From the first day of the seventh month they began to offer burnt offerings to the LORD, although the foundation of the temple of the LORD had not been laid. (Ezra 3:1-6)

Nehemiah recorded that sweeping revival also took place in Israel that same day as Ezra rehearsed God's law in the ears of the people (see Nehemiah 7:73; 8:13).

The time between Rosh Hashanah and Yom Kippur was considered ten days of repentance, or the Days of Awe.

According to Talmudic custom, it is believed that God reviews the books in these ten days to see if judgment will come to the person on the Day of Atonement. These ten days are believed to be the last chance to repent before God's judgment is finalized for the coming year, since three books are opened on Rosh Hashanah: the Book of Life for the wicked, the Book of Life for the righteous, and the Book of Life for the in-between.

Again, according to the Talmudic customs, as God reviews the deeds of mankind for the past year, He inscribes the name of every individual in one of these books. Judgment is final and irrevocable—they will have life cut short in the coming year. Those recorded in the Book of Life for the righteous will be mercifully granted another year of life and prosperity by the Lord. For the remainder—for those not written in either of the books—the sealing of their fate is deferred and hangs in the balance until Yom Kippur. If one sincerely repents during the Days of Awe, God will grant them life until the following Day of Atonement.

Let me repeat that the three books are from the Talmud, not the Old Testament. However, we do know that Moses referred to such a book in Exodus 32:32-33, *"'Yet now, if You will forgive their sin—but if not, I pray, blot me out of Your book which You have written.' And the LORD said to Moses, 'Whoever has sinned against Me, I will blot him out of My book.'"* King David also said, *"Let them be blotted out of the book of the living, and not be written with the righteous"* (Psalm 69:28).

What we do know from the Old Testament was that the ten days from Rosh Hashanah and Yom Kippur were to be (and still are) a time of repentance. Even today, during this season you will find Jews sitting beside water—oceans, streams, rivers, pools—asking God to cast their sin into the water. (See Micah 7:18-20; Psalm 33; 118:5-9; 130; Isaiah 11:9.) Micah 7:19 tells us: *"He will again have compassion on us, and will subdue our iniquities. You will cast all our sins into the depths of the sea."*

Then and now, the Feast of Trumpets is Israel's dark day. It occurs at the new moon, when the primary night light of the heavens is darkened, as Zephaniah penned:

> *The great day of the LORD is near;*
> *It is near and hastens quickly.*
> *The noise of the day of the LORD is bitter;*
> *There the mighty men shall cry out.*
> *That day is a day of wrath,*
> *A day of trouble and distress,*
> *A day of devastation and desolation,*
> *A day of darkness and gloominess,*
> *A day of clouds and thick darkness,*
> *A day of trumpet and alarm*
> *Against the fortified cities*
> *And against the high towers.* (Zephaniah 1:14-16)

Is it any wonder that Israel still knows the Feast of Trumpets as the Day of the Lord?

THE DAY OF ATONEMENT

Yom Kippur, the second of those days, is the Jewish name for the Day of Atonement. It is one of the *Yamim Noraim* (Hebrew for "Days of Awe"), and it is considered the holiest day of the Jewish year. It occurs in the seventh month (Tishri), the tenth day; and the Feast of Tabernacles begins on Tishri 15. This is the most solemn of all feasts, and the Day of Atonement was (and still is) the time for national and sanctuary cleansing. The Hebrew name for this holy day comes from the word *kaphar*, which means "covering."

In Hebrew, *Yom* means "day" and *Kippur* means "to pardon, or condone." *Atonement*, the English word, has the same meaning, "to make amends or to reconcile." It was on Yom Kippur, the Day of Atonement, that a covering, or sacrifice, was made for the previous year's sin.

On this day, sacrifices were offered for atonement, or reconciliation (to become "at one"). The special and peculiar offerings were two goats. Divine instructions were given to the high priest. Leviticus 16 outlines these instructions:

> *And the LORD said to Moses: "Tell Aaron your brother not to come at just any time into the Holy Place inside the veil, before the mercy seat which is on the ark, lest he die; for I will appear in the cloud above the mercy seat.*
>
> *Thus Aaron shall come into the Holy Place: with the blood of a young bull as a sin offering, and of a ram as a burnt offering. He shall put the holy linen tunic and the linen trousers on his body; he shall be girded with a linen sash, and with the linen turban he shall be attired. These are holy garments. Therefore he shall wash his body in water, and put them on. And he shall take from the congregation of the children of Israel two kids of the goats as a sin offering, and one ram as a burnt offering.*

Aaron shall offer the bull as a sin offering, which is for himself, and make atonement for himself and for his house. He shall take the two goats and present them before the Lord at the door of the tabernacle of meeting. Then Aaron shall cast lots for the two goats: one lot for the LORD and the other lot for the scapegoat. And Aaron shall bring the goat on which the LORD'S lot fell, and offer it as a sin offering. But the goat on which the lot fell to be the scapegoat shall be presented alive before the LORD, to make atonement upon it, and to let it go as the scapegoat into the wilderness.

And Aaron shall bring the bull of the sin offering, which is for himself, and make atonement for himself and for his house, and shall kill the bull as the sin offering which is for himself. Then he shall take a censer full of burning coals of fire from the altar before the LORD, with his hands full of sweet incense beaten fine, and bring it inside the veil. And he shall put the incense on the fire before the LORD, that the cloud of incense may cover the mercy seat that is on the Testimony, lest he die. He shall take some of the blood of the bull and sprinkle it with his finger on the mercy seat on the east side; and before the mercy seat he shall sprinkle some of the blood with his finger seven times.

Then he shall kill the goat of the sin offering, which is for the people, bring its blood inside the veil, do with that blood as he did with the blood of the bull, and sprinkle it on the mercy seat and before the mercy seat. So he shall make atonement for the Holy Place." (Leviticus 16:2-16)

The Lord commanded Aaron not to come into the Holiest of Holies at all times, but only on this one day of the year. Even then he was to enter only with the blood of the sacrifice, the golden censor, and his hands full of sweet incense. It was only then that he could bring the offering within the veil.

Additional passages detail the biblical observance of the Day of Atonement:

> And the LORD spoke to Moses, saying: "Also the tenth day of this seventh month shall be the Day of Atonement. It shall be a holy convocation for you; you shall afflict your souls, and offer an offering made by fire to the LORD. And you shall do no work on that same day, for it is the Day of Atonement, to make atonement for you before the LORD your God. For any person who is not afflicted in soul on that same day shall be cut off from his people. And any person who does any work on that same day, that person I will destroy from among his people. You shall do no manner of work; it shall be a statute forever throughout your generations in all your dwellings. It shall be to you a sabbath of solemn rest, and you shall afflict your souls; on the ninth day of the month at evening, from evening to evening, you shall celebrate your sabbath." (Leviticus 23:26-32)

> On the tenth day of this seventh month you shall have a holy convocation. You shall afflict your souls; you shall not do any work. You shall present a burnt offering to the LORD as a

sweet aroma: one young bull, one ram, and seven lambs in their first year. Be sure they are without blemish. Their grain offering shall be of fine flour mixed with oil: three-tenths of an ephah for the bull, two-tenths for the one ram, and one-tenth for each of the seven lambs; also one kid of the goats as a sin offering, besides the sin offering for atonement, the regular burnt offering with its grain offering, and their drink offerings. (Numbers 29:7-11)

At this sacred time of the year, the high priest would take the blood sacrifice of animals—innocent animals such as a year-old lamb—and cover the ark of the covenant with it by sprinkling it on the ark seven times.

One goat was slain, and the other—a scapegoat—was taken to the wilderness at the hand of a man, bearing away the sins of the people. On this solemn day, once a year, the high priest entered into the holiest of all, within the veil, with the blood of the sin offering, and he sprinkled the blood on the mercy seat.

This Day of Atonement blood offering for sin brought about the cleansing of all sins, all iniquities, and all transgressions. All—the priests, the sanctuary, and the entire nation of Israel—experienced the atonement of the blood, and this atonement reconciled them to God.

In Leviticus we read:

Also the tenth day of this seventh month shall be the Day of Atonement. It shall be a holy convocation for you; you shall

afflict your souls, and offer an offering made by fire to the
LORD. And you shall do no work on that same day, for it is
the Day of Atonement, to make atonement for you before the
LORD your God. (Leviticus 23:27-28)

Throughout all of the instructions, it is important to note six significant and specific elements:

Fasting—The Day of Atonement is unique because it is the only holy day in which fasting was required. This was such a strict requirement that anyone who failed to do so would be banished from the rest. By definition, the Day of Atonement was a specified time to fast from sunup to sundown.

Changing of the Garments—On the Day of Atonement Aaron laid aside his garments of glory and beauty: *"And you shall make holy garments for Aaron your brother, for glory and for beauty"* (Exodus 28:2), to don linen garments: *"He shall put the holy linen tunic and the linen trousers on his body; he shall be girded with a linen sash, and with the linen turban he shall be attired. These are holy garments. Therefore he shall wash his body in water, and put them on"* (Leviticus 16:4). After making the atonement in the sanctuary and washing the holy place, he took off the holy garments of linen and changed back into the garments of glory and beauty. Even today, Sephardic Jews (Jews of Spanish, Portuguese, and North African descent) refer to this holiday as the "White Fast," and many Jews have the custom of wearing only white clothing on this day, to symbolize their "white" purity from sin.

The Precious Blood—First, Aaron came in with the blood of the bullock, which he sprinkled seven times on the mercy seat.

Incense—Incense always speaks of prayer and worship, and as Aaron entered within the veil, placing the incense on the fiery coals of the censor, a cloud of incense ascended, covering the ark of glory.

Washing of Water—On the Day of Atonement, also, there was the special washing of water in preparation for the sacrificial offering. Aaron washed before he entered the sanctuary, then washed again in the holy place after the sanctuary had been cleansed (see Leviticus 16:4, 24).

The Scapegoat—The *Azazel* goat, or scapegoat, was taken out into the wilderness after having had all of the sins of the Israelites ceremonially placed upon it.

Even today, the observance of the Day of Atonement is held with utmost importance among the majority of Jews, even those who may not strictly observe other holidays. Attendance in synagogues on Yom Kippur is much greater on this day than the rest of the year. In Israel, for example, on that day there are no public festivities, eating, television, or public transportation. Even the airports are closed to traffic.

It is an exceptional day each year. According to ancient customs, during the evening prayers marking the beginning of the Day of Atonement, many men wear a four-cornered prayer garment called a *tallit*. This is the sole evening service during the year when the prayer shawl is worn. Many wear white on Yom Kippur, a symbol of purity and forgiveness of sins. Married men often elect to wear a white shroud, the robe in which the dead are buried, which is called a *kittel* or *kitel*.[1] These evening services begin with the *Kol Nidre*, which must be prayed before the sun sets, followed by additional prayers.

The morning of Yom Kippur begins with *selichot*, prayers of petition for forgiveness. These are followed by the *mussaf*, an added prayer, then the *mincha*, an afternoon prayer. The *ne'ilah* prayer, which follows, is used only on the Day of Atonement. Then the *Sheman Yisrael* and the blowing of the *ShofarHaGadol*, known in English as the Great Trumpet, signal the end of the fast.[2]

Customarily on the Day of Atonement, passages are read from Leviticus 16 (in the morning service) and Leviticus 18 (during the afternoon prayers). The book of Jonah is read in the afternoon *haftarah*. During each prayer, the *vidduy*, or confession, is included.

The Day of Atonement was (and still is) a set-aside, divinely assigned day of prohibitions from all forms of work. If one did not heed the call, he would be served the death penalty. On this day, the people were to repent of their sins during the past year and to fast in symbolism of their true repentance. This is important to remember, especially as a foundation for the remainder of this book.

THE FEAST OF TABERNACLES

The third feast of the Tabernacles season, and the seventh (and final) of God's holy days, was the most joyful and festive of all of Israel's feasts. It is also the most prominent feast, mentioned more often in Scripture than any of the other feasts. This feast also observed as a historical backdrop for the teaching of Jesus in John, chapters 7–9.

The Feast of Tabernacles is known by at least two names: Sukkoth and Tabernacles. *Tabernacle* comes from the Latin *tabernaculum* and means "booth or hut." Every year when all the males stood before the Lord the third time, Israel would build booths or huts and celebrate for seven days. It was also called the Feast of Ingathering.

Exodus 23:16 refers to this time: *"And the Feast of Harvest, the firstfruits of your labors which you have sown in the field; and the Feast of Ingathering at the end of the year, when you have gathered in the fruit of your labors from the field."*

Exodus 34:22 also points to this feast: *"And you shall observe the Feast of Weeks, of the firstfruits of wheat harvest, and the Feast of Ingathering at the year's end."* This feast was to be observed after all the crops had been harvested and gathered.

God wanted to see evidence that they remembered how He supplied their needs during the forty years in the wilderness and to commemorate God's present goodness and provision with the completion of the harvest.

We find in three portions of Scripture an outline of the biblical observance of the Feast of Tabernacles:

- There people were to live in booths and rejoice before the Lord with branches (Leviticus 23:33-43).

- There were to be many daily sacrificial offerings (Numbers 29:12-39).

- In the sabbatical year, the Law was to be read publicly during the time of this Feast (Deuteronomy 31:10-13).

During the Feast of Tabernacles, the people brought tithes and offerings to the temple, for they were not to appear before the Lord empty-handed: *"Three times a year all your males shall appear before the LORD your God in the place which He chooses: at the Feast of Unleavened Bread, at the Feast of Weeks, and at the Feast of Tabernacles; and they shall not appear before the LORD empty-handed"* (Deuteronomy 16:16). This is so very important. God waits for us to give Him an offering on this special feast day.

Remember, the word *feast* embodies the meaning of appointment. God has created an appointment with man. During the Feast of Tabernacles, there were seven days of festivities, joy, and offerings. The first day's offering was to be one goat, fourteen lambs, two rams, and a number of bullocks. Each succeeding day the offering was to be decreased by one animal.

This feast is significant throughout the Word of God. Solomon dedicated the newly built temple to the Lord during the Feast of Tabernacles (2 Chronicles 5:3). The Shekinah glory of the Lord descended from heaven to light the fire on the altar and filled the Holy of Holies (1 Kings 8; 2 Chronicles 7:1-10).

During this time of ingathering, notice that God—not man—created the season of rains. It is interesting to note that even today Israel receives most of its precipitation each year starting in November and ending sometime in March (Gregorian calendar). These rains are important to the land of Israel so the soil can be refreshed and new crops can be grown for the new season.

LOOKING FORWARD

Dr. Eugene Merrill, in his timeless textbook, *An Historical Survey of the Old Testament*, points to the overriding need of a foundational understanding of the seven feasts, certainly including the Day of Atonement:

> Mosaic Law, then, with all its aspects and categories still was nothing more than the framework in which Israel expressed the fact that it was a covenant people and that it desired to worship the God who had called them and made of them a nation. The regulations, the statutes, the ritual—all were purposeful expressions of the covenant faith; though completely meaningless in and of themselves, they were absolutely indispensable for that people and at that time. They were not inventions of an ancient Semitic mind, but Divine revelation from their God.[3]

Those who correctly observed each feast received supernatural blessings. Just as God did with the children of Israel, He is poised to pour out these seven blessings upon your life, as you will see in chapter 3 and beyond.

First, however, in chapter 2 let's put to rest, once and for all, whether Christians should observe these commemoration seasons, especially the Day of Atonement.

2

CHRISTIANS CELEBRATING THE DAY OF ATONEMENT?

Alas and did my Saviour bleed?
And did my Sovereign die?
Would he devote that sacred head
For such a worm as I?

Was it for crimes that I have done,
He groaned upon the tree?
Amazing pity! Grace unknown!
And love beyond degree.

Well might the sun in darkness hide
And shut His glories in,
When Christ, the great Redeemer, died
For Man the creature's sin.

—ISAAC WATTS

All of the ancient feasts were given specifically to point the nation of Israel toward the time when the Messiah would come to teach a

New Covenant, no longer just with physical rituals, but to gain the privilege of a personal, spiritual fellowship with the Father.

Jesus offered Himself as a sacrifice for our sins, "once and for all," so we don't have to live under the curse of the law. We are free to serve Him under the New Covenant. However, you cannot fully understand the New Covenant until you grasp the meaning of the Old Covenant. Neither can you truly appreciate all Jesus did for each of us on the cross until you peer closely into the meaning of the feasts of Israel.

Each of these feasts should be significant to Christians today because they individually point us to the steps in God's plan for salvation, fellowship, and eternal life. These principles are for all the feasts, which are given not just to the children of Israel, but to Christians today who have been grafted into God's family through the Savior's sacrifice. We should study and observe these feasts, asking the Father for wisdom in understanding the truths in each feast. There is a wealth of information to study. Our lives can be revolutionized through these feasts. The secret to seeing God's truth at work in your life comes through having spiritual eyes and obedience to the wisdom that He imparts to you as He seeks to impact your life forever!

This is what the Master meant when He told His followers, *"Think not that I am come to destroy the law, or the prophets: I am not come to destroy, but to fulfill"* (Matthew 5:17, KJV). Obviously, the Old Covenant was given for a specific purpose that we, His followers today, could more fully understand the New Covenant.

JESUS OBSERVED THE FEASTS

A few years ago everybody, it seemed, was wearing WWJD on wristbands, T-shirts, belts, caps, and even tattoos! It was a good question made extremely popular over a hundred years ago by Charles Sheldon, pastor of Central Congregational Church in Topeka, Kansas, with a series of unusual sermons that was a continued fictitious story, one chapter to be given out each week at church about what happened in the lives of various persons with different backgrounds and vocations when they dared to follow Christ's example in everyday life. The sermon series became a best-selling, classic book, *In His Steps*, and today continues to urge people of all backgrounds to ask, "What would Jesus do?" It is a fitting question concerning the feasts.

According to the Word of God, our Lord Jesus celebrated the feasts. He observed Passover from the time He was twelve years old (Luke 2:41-42) until His final Passover (Matthew 26). Likewise, He observed the Day of Atonement (as part of the Tabernacles season), recorded the memorable passage from the Gospel of John:

> *After these things Jesus walked in Galilee; for He did not want to walk in Judea, because the Jews sought to kill Him. Now the Jews' Feast of Tabernacles was at hand.... Now about the middle of the feast Jesus went up into the temple and taught. And the Jews marveled, saying, "How does this Man know letters, having never studied?" Jesus answered them and said, "My doctrine is not Mine, but His who sent Me." (John 7:1-2, 14-16)*

Early believers followed Christ's example. In Acts 27, Paul was being taken by ship as a prisoner to Rome from Lycia. A fierce storm arose. Paul and 276 other men, many of whom were violent criminals, were suddenly adrift on a ship that was tossing and turning on the violent sea. They remained on the ship fourteen days in this terrible storm.

During that time, Paul realized that the Day of Atonement was approaching (see Leviticus 23:27-29; Acts 27:9). He was not only a valiant warrior for the name of Jesus Christ, but he also had a strong Jewish faith that had been instilled in him by years of scholarly pursuit. It was the Tabernacles season, just before winter (Acts 27:12), because the Day of Atonement fast is mentioned (verse 9).

In the midst of this time, Paul admonished the captain of the boat that much danger lay ahead, and there would be much hurt and damage. When hope was gone, Paul spoke up again:

> *But after long abstinence from food, then Paul stood in the midst of them and said, "Men, you should have listened to me, and not have sailed from Crete and incurred this disaster and loss. And now I urge you to take heart, for there will be no loss of life among you, but only of the ship. For there stood by me this night an angel of the God to whom I belong and whom I serve, saying, 'Do not be afraid, Paul; you must be brought before Caesar; and indeed God has granted you all those who sail with you.' Therefore take heart, men, for I believe God that it will be just as it was told me." (Acts 27:21-25)*

Paul honored the Day of Atonement before God, even near the end of his life and in prisoner's chains. God blessed him—and all those who were on the ship with him—by sparing his life.

THE OLD AND THE NEW

Our Savior, as did the early believers, honored the seven feasts, God's own holy days. They followed the specific instructions given for their observance. They openly observed these appointed times, knowing that the sequence and time of each of these feasts had been carefully orchestrated by God Himself.

Then and now, these three feast seasons—Passover, Pentecost, and Tabernacles—represent the three major links between God and His covenant children. In the seven great feasts of the Lord—Passover, Unleavened Bread, Firstfruits, Pentecost, Trumpets, Atonement, and Tabernacles—all point back to what God did to establish His covenant with the children of Israel. All, likewise, point to Christ the Savior.

Today, these feasts are filled with meaning for believers.

The Feast of the Passover Points to Christ Our Passover

"Therefore purge out the old leaven, that you may be a new lump, since you truly are unleavened. For indeed Christ, our Passover, was sacrificed for us" (1 Corinthians 5:7). Passover speaks of redemption through Jesus, the Lamb of God.

The Feast of Unleavened Bread Points to Jesus, Our Bread of Life

"And Jesus said to them, 'I am the bread of life. He who comes to Me shall never hunger, and he who believes in Me shall never thirst.'" (John 6:35). The Feast of Unleavened Bread speaks of sanctification—Jesus's body would not decay in the tomb.

The Feast of the Firstfruits Guides Us to the Savior

> *But now Christ is risen from the dead, and has become the firstfruits of those who have fallen asleep. For since by man came death, by Man also came the resurrection of the dead. For as in Adam all die, even so in Christ all shall be made alive. But each one in his own order: Christ the firstfruits, afterward those who are Christ's at His coming.* (1 Corinthians 15:20-23)

The Feast of Firstfruits speaks of resurrection—Jesus was the Firstfruits of the brethren and rose from the grave.

The Feast of Pentecost Shows That the Holy Spirit Bore Witness of Jesus the Savior at Pentecost

> *When the Day of Pentecost had fully come, they were all with one accord in one place. And suddenly there came a sound from heaven, as of a rushing mighty wind, and it filled the whole house where they were sitting. Then there appeared to them divided tongues, as of fire, and one sat upon each of them. And they were all filled with the Holy Spirit and began to speak with other tongues, as the Spirit gave them utterance.* (Acts 2:1-4)

This came in direct fulfillment of the prophetic words given to His followers just before the Savior's ascension into heaven: *"But you shall receive power when the Holy Spirit has come upon you; and you shall be witnesses to Me in Jerusalem, and in all Judea and Samaria, and to the end of the earth"* (Acts 1:8).

The Feast of Weeks speaks of origination—the new Church Age, New Covenant, new Body of Christ. This is also known as Pentecost.

The Feast of Trumpets Reveals the Soon-Coming Savior

We are to look for His appearance: *"For the Lord Himself will descend from heaven with a shout, with the voice of an archangel, and with the trumpet of God. And the dead in Christ will rise first"* (1 Thessalonians 4:16). Since ancient times, the shofar (ram's horn) has sounded to call assembly, to signal sacrifice, or to panic the enemy in battle. On the day when the Lord returns for His church, the trumpet will sound to signal one of history's greatest moments!

The Feast of Atonement Teaches How the Word Became Flesh

> *But God demonstrates His own love toward us, in that while we were still sinners, Christ died for us. Much more then, having now been justified by His blood, we shall be saved from wrath through Him. For if when we were enemies we were reconciled to God through the death of His Son, much more, having been reconciled, we shall be saved by His life. And not only that, but we also rejoice in God through our Lord Jesus Christ, through whom we have now received the reconciliation.*

Therefore, just as through one man sin entered the world, and death through sin, and thus death spread to all men, because all sinned—(For until the law sin was in the world, but sin is not imputed when there is no law. Nevertheless death reigned from Adam to Moses, even over those who had not sinned according to the likeness of the transgression of Adam, who is a type of Him who was to come. But the free gift is not like the offense. For if by the one man's offense many died, much more the grace of God and the gift by the grace of the one Man, Jesus Christ, abounded to many.) (Romans 5:8-15)

The Feast of Tabernacles Shows the Creator's Plan to Send Jesus to Establish Fellowship with Us, His Authority, Ownership, and Reign

"And the Word became flesh and dwelt among us, and we beheld His glory, the glory as of the only begotten of the Father, full of grace and truth" (John 1:14).

Each of these feasts speaks of the Messiah, Jesus of Nazareth. Through each of the feasts, especially the Passover, it is clearly evident how all that follows in the Old Covenant pointed toward the Cross and beyond.

THE ATONEMENT, THEN AND NOW

Christ Jesus is the fulfillment of all of the seven feasts. In chapter 1, I discussed six (of the many) significant and specific elements of the Day of Atonement. In each, Christ was also our example.

Fasting

The Day of Atonement is unique because it is the only holy day in which fasting was required. There is no greater example of fasting than our wonderful Lord. The first-century Christians, including the apostle Paul, followed His example by observing the Day of Atonement (Acts 27:9). As Christ's followers, we know that fasting reveals a heart of repentance. Fasting brings readiness for atonement, forgiveness, and blessing.

Changing of the Garments

On the Day of Atonement Aaron laid aside his garments of glory and beauty: *"And you shall make holy garments for Aaron your brother, for glory and for beauty"* (Exodus 28:2), to don linen garments: *"He shall put the holy linen tunic and the linen trousers on his body; he shall be girded with a linen sash, and with the linen turban he shall be attired. These are holy garments. Therefore he shall wash his body in water, and put them on"* (Leviticus 16:4). After making the atonement in the sanctuary and washing the Holy Place, he took off the holy garments of linen and changed back into the garments of glory and beauty. How wonderfully the Lord Jesus fulfilled this type in Himself, for He laid aside His reputation, emptying Himself of His glory, and took on the likeness of men:

> *Let this mind be in you which was also in Christ Jesus, who, being in the form of God, did not consider it robbery to be equal with God, but made Himself of no reputation, taking the form of a bondservant, and coming in the likeness of men. And being found in appearance as a man, He humbled Himself and became obedient to the point of death, even the death of the cross. Therefore*

God also has highly exalted Him and given Him the name which is above every name, that at the name of Jesus every knee should bow, of those in heaven, and of those on earth, and of those under the earth, and that every tongue should confess that Jesus Christ is Lord, to the glory of God the Father. (Philippians 2:5-11)

Later on, God highly exalted Him, clothed Him with glory and honor, and gave Him a name above all names! Likewise, on that soon-coming, glorious day, believers will also experience a change of garments when we put off this corruption and put on incorruption.

The Precious Blood

First, Aaron came in with the blood of the bullock, which he sprinkled seven times on the mercy seat. This was fulfilled in the perfect work of the Cross when the blood of Jesus was shed for you and me—at Gethsemane when *"His sweat became like great drops of blood falling down to the ground"* (Luke 22:44), when the crown of thorns was placed upon His precious head (John 19:2), when the soldiers hit His face (Matthew 26:67), when His beard was plucked off (Isaiah 50:6), when He was scourged with the whip (Matthew 27:26), when He was nailed to the cross (Matthew 27:35; Luke 24:39-40; John 20:27), and when His side was pierced by the sword (John 19:34). The author of Hebrews tells us:

But Christ came as High Priest of the good things to come, with the greater and more perfect tabernacle not made with hands, that is, not of this creation. Not with the blood of goats and calves, but with His own blood He entered the

Most Holy Place once for all, having obtained eternal redemption. For if the blood of bulls and goats and the ashes of a heifer, sprinkling the unclean, sanctifies for the purifying of the flesh, how much more shall the blood of Christ, who through the eternal Spirit offered Himself without spot to God, cleanse your conscience from dead works to serve the living God? (Hebrews 9:11-14)

The precious blood, shed on the Day of Atonement and fulfilled through Christ Jesus, also speaks of our perfection, because of the atonement we have received through our Savior's shed blood, on that glorious day when we enter into His presence!

Incense

Incense always speaks of prayer and worship, and as Aaron entered within the veil, placing the incense on the fiery coals of the censor, a cloud of incense ascended, covering the ark of glory.

The incense also speaks of worship, for the Scripture says in Psalm 29:2, *"Give unto the LORD the glory due unto his name; worship the LORD in the beauty of holiness."* This will be fulfilled when we stand before Him in heaven, perfect and holy, praising Him forever for all He has done.

Washing of Water

On the Day of Atonement there was also the special washing of water in preparation for the sacrificial offering. Aaron washed before he entered the sanctuary, then washed again in the Holy Place after the sanctuary had been cleansed (Leviticus 16:4, 24). This will be fulfilled on that glorious day when we, cleansed by the water of the Word, will be presented perfect to Him: *"Christ also loved the church and gave Himself for her, that He might sanctify and cleanse her with the washing of water by the word, that He might present her to Himself a glorious church, not having spot or wrinkle or any such thing, but that she should be holy and without blemish"* (Ephesians 5:25-27).

The Scapegoat

The *Azazel* goat, or scapegoat, was taken out into the wilderness after having had all of the sins of the Israelites ceremonially placed upon it. It was done by the high priest after returning from inside the Holy of Holies. The scapegoat was a symbol of our sinful condemnation. No longer do we need a high priest to go into the Holy of Holies once a year to intercede for our sins, nor do we need a scapegoat. Jesus fulfilled our greatest need, for He died in our place.

Then as now, Jesus is our High Priest (Hebrews 9:11). He is our atonement. He is our Mediator and Intercessor. Hebrews 7:25 states, *"Wherefore he is able also to save them to the uttermost that come unto God by him, seeing he ever liveth to make intercession for them"* (KJV).

Richard Booker, in his excellent book, *Jesus in the Feasts of Israel*, wrote:

> Jesus fulfilled the spiritual aspects of the Day of Atonement when He went into the heavenly holy of holies with his own blood which He shed for the sins of the world. We have been forgiven and made clean once

and for all by the blood of Jesus Christ. The blood of Jesus did what the blood of bulls and goats could never do. It didn't just cover our sins, it took them away to be remembered no more. [1]

Granted, even though God forgives all sins when a person receives Him into one's heart, we still need a continual cleansing. We must repent of sins to maintain close fellowship with the Father. Still, the blood of Jesus Christ, shed once on Calvary, was sufficient to atone and cover all the sins of mankind from that point forward.

FULFILLMENT

In the Old Covenant, the Day of Atonement was the most solemn of all days throughout Israel. The atonement was fulfilled completely through our wonderful Lord Jesus when He hung on Calvary's cross and said, *"It is finished!"* (John 19:30).

It is important that we, as blood-washed believers, understand and observe the Day of Atonement today, for someday soon the feast will be fulfilled in us, the church, when we stand before Him. We see in part today, but on that day we will know the fullness of the manifestation of the power of His blood. The power of sin will be destroyed forever. We will stand perfect before Him and His throne, free at last from all iniquity, transgressions, and death.

The word *atonement* means "reconciliation." The Day of Atonement was fulfilled in Christ Jesus when He died on Calvary's cross. Christians can look toward the day when we will receive full reconcilement between God and His people. The most solemn of all days will be turned into a celebration as we see the full manifestation of the atonement—as we will see the final fulfillment of all seven feasts!

The Passover has been observed historically by the children of Israel, fulfilled through the shed blood of the Lamb of God, and applied by the church. Unleavened Bread was observed in Israel as they ate bread without leaven, was fulfilled in Christ when He destroyed sin on the cross, and is applied when each believer walks away from sin. The Firstfruit was observed by Jews when they actually brought the sheaf of the harvest to the altar, it was fulfilled in the Savior when He rose from the dead, and it is applied in Christians who walk in newness of life. After crossing the Red Sea, we move on to Pentecost, observed by the children of Israel as the Feast of Weeks, fulfilled in Christ when He sent the Holy Spirit, and applied to believers who are baptized in the Holy Ghost. These have all been observed, all fulfilled, all applied.

However, the final three have not been. Trumpets is symbolically observed by Jews, yet they have not yet come into the fullness of that feast, for it speaks of the re-gathering of Israel. That started in 1948, and the shophar was blown, but it has not been completed. The regathering of Israel will happen when all the tribes of Israel come back home. They are still coming back home. When the trumpets sound to signal the rapture of the church, the Feast of Trumpets will begin, fully complete and observed. It will be applied to each believer as we are changed in the twinkling of an eye.

Likewise, the Day of Atonement has not been fully observed or fulfilled. It is symbolically observed in Israel. It has been fulfilled in Christ. It has been applied to the church. God's wisdom and plan ordained that the Day of Atonement was fulfilled when Christ offered His shed blood. Yet the application of the atonement is only partial until the same blood that cleansed the church also cleanses the children of Israel. The church has experienced it, but the chosen nation of God, the ones who gave us the oracles, have not. And even though believers today have experienced the cleansing of the blood, the blessed power of Christ's shed blood, we have not experienced the fullness of atonement yet. We are still in imperfect human bodies. Yet one of these days we shall be thoroughly atoned because the Savior's blood will remove death, the last enemy to be destroyed.

Yes, it was fulfilled when the Messiah died on the cross, then ascended as the great High Priest walked into heaven itself and presented His own shed blood as an offering (Hebrews 9:7-14). Yet the Day of Atonement for the church will be the fullest manifestation of the power of the blood of Christ. It will bring the church to perfection, marking an end of all iniquity, all transgressions, and all sins for the church.

Zechariah 3:9 declares: *"For behold the stone that I have laid before Joshua; upon one stone shall be seven eyes: behold, I will engrave the graving thereof, saith the* LORD *of hosts, and I will remove the iniquity of that land in one day"* (KJV). This will happen in one day! Now, that one day may be a literal twenty-four-hour period, or it may be an indefinite season of time. We must rightly divide the Word. The Day of Atonement has been partially fulfilled, for Christ walked into heaven, and the blood has been applied to believers. But it has not been applied yet for all the Jewish people.

If it were complete, even for us, we would be sinless as Christ was. We'd never fall short. The blood cleanses us, but the power of death is still working in our bodies. We still must fight sin. The apostle Paul even said, *"Therefore do not let sin reign in your mortal body, that you should obey it in its lusts. And do not present your members as instruments of unrighteousness to sin, but present yourselves to God as being alive from the dead, and your members as instruments of righteousness to God"* (Romans 6:12-13).

We are not to let sin win, but the battle rages every day. We were conceived in sin. We have iniquity, or the perverseness of spirit. We sin, or go astray, missing the mark. We transgress, or rebel, and are lawless. We are unclean, defiled and polluted. Yet He gave Himself our atonement for all those horrible things:

> *Surely He has borne our griefs*
> *And carried our sorrows;*
> *Yet we esteemed Him stricken,*
> *Smitten by God, and afflicted.*
> *But He was wounded for our transgressions,*
> *He was bruised for our iniquities;*
> *The chastisement for our peace was upon Him,*
> *And by His stripes we are healed.*
> *All we like sheep have gone astray;*
> *We have turned, every one, to his own way;*
>
> *And the* Lord *has laid on Him the iniquity of us all.*
> (Isaiah 53:4-6)

Until we reach heaven's shore, we must be cleansed all the time. Yet the great news is that one day we will be cleansed forever. We will never have to say, "Please wash me again." We can walk in the presence of God, holy and blameless.

When that atonement is full and complete, when on that day it is fully applied to believers, than all iniquity, all sin and all uncleanness will be removed once and for all. The ultimate Day of Atonement will bring about full reconciliation for believers with our Creator and Redeemer. That time is soon approaching!

Should Christians Observe the Feasts?

Many Christians have been taught that the Day of Atonement, as with all seven feasts, is an outdated Jewish observance, done away with at Jesus's death. But why did Jesus Christ keep the feasts? Why did He encourage His followers to attend and observe the feasts? Why did the first-century Christians continue to commemorate these holy days?

The reason is clear: Jesus offered Himself as a sacrifice for our sins, *"once and for all,"* so we don't have to live under the curse of the law. We are free to serve Him under the New Covenant. However, no one can fully comprehend the New Covenant until grasping the meaning of the Old Covenant. Neither can someone understand what Jesus Christ did for each of us on the cross until peering closely into the meaning of the feasts of Israel, especially the Day of Atonement.

All of the feasts offer supernatural truth, which the Holy Spirit uses to help you understand what He wants to do through you right now. In addition, the feasts are a shadow of things to come to help us understand prophecy better and be prepared for what is to come. The feasts offer a wealth of information upon which we can build our lives. Best of all, the feasts reveal heavenly things, giving us an eternal hope.

And, as you will begin to see in the next chapter, God has provided—through the holy days, specifically the Day of Atonement—seven very special Joel 2 blessings which can impact your life today!

3

SEVEN BLESSINGS UNLEASHED IN YOUR LIFE

Do not think that I came to destroy the Law or the Prophets. I did not come to destroy but to fulfill.

—MATTHEW 5:17

Yes, Jesus died for our sins. Yes, Jesus made a new covenant. Yes, His death, burial, and resurrection fulfilled the Law and the prophets. However, His new covenant, brought about by dying on the cross, delivered us from the curse of sin.

Why, then, would any of us knowingly live under the curse of sin? More to the point, why wouldn't we want to access every single blessing that God has made available to us?

In Galatians Paul declares:

Just as Abraham "believed God, and it was accounted to him for righteousness." Therefore know that only those who are of faith are sons of Abraham. And the Scripture, foreseeing that God would justify the Gentiles by faith, preached the gospel

49

to Abraham beforehand, saying, "In you all the nations shall be blessed." So then those who are of faith are blessed with believing Abraham.

For as many as are of the works of the law are under the curse; for it is written, "Cursed is everyone who does not continue in all things which are written in the book of the law, to do them." But that no one is justified by the law in the sight of God is evident, for "the just shall live by faith." Yet the law is not of faith, but "the man who does them shall live by them."

Christ has redeemed us from the curse of the law, having become a curse for us (for it is written, "Cursed is everyone who hangs on a tree"), that the blessing of Abraham might come upon the Gentiles in Christ Jesus, that we might receive the promise of the Spirit through faith. (Galatians 3:6-14)

His blood did not, as in the Old Testament, simply cover our sins. His blood remitted, or did away with, our sins. His sacrificial death takes away our sins, gives us a brand-new life, and takes care of our future eternally with Jesus Christ in the heavenlies.

However, we cannot simply disregard the Old Testament. In fact, paying attention to those things commanded by God to His people before Calvary puts "mile-markers" into our life, making us aware of God's blessings available to every believer during the most important seasons.

TURMOIL AND TROUBLE

Have you noticed that the days leading up to the fall of the year are a particularly troublesome time? Very often, during the "dog days" of

August and into September so much turmoil happens, seemingly for no reason. Webster even defines the "dog days of summer" this way: "the period between early July and early September when the hot sultry weather of summer usually occurs in the northern hemisphere; and a period of stagnation or inactivity."

It is interesting that there are as many references to the origination of "dog days" as books or online sites that you research. Apparently the term *caniculares dies* (days of the dog) was first used by the ancient Greeks, Romans, and Egyptians, in reference to the *Canis Major* (bigger dog) constellation, where the *Canis Majoris* (Sirius) star is found. Sirius is the brightest star seen from Earth, especially during the dog days, or hottest time of the year. Similar terms are used in many cultures, including the Spanish who call this period during late summer and early autumn *la canicula*, from the Latin root *canis* (dog).[1]

The appearance of Sirius—during the time corresponding to our mid-August each year—was blamed for many calamities. Traditionally, many believed that the scorching heat from the Dog Star actually increased the sun's heat. In addition, the ancient Egyptians observed that the Nile Delta would begin flooding each year shortly after Sirius was easily viewed during the time that corresponds to our mid-August.[2]

Flooding? Heat? Either way, "dog days" hardly describe the most wonderful days of the year.

During these days leading up to the fall season, the whole earth seems to groan, as if going through birth pains. History is filled with numerous examples:

- Herod—during the Atonement season—ordered the murders of more than 60,000 male children, aged two and younger.

- It should be no surprise that many wars have more often than not been started during the months of August and September, running through the Tabernacles season and Day of Atonement.

- During the fateful September of 1939, World War II officially began on the first day of the month with the invasion of Poland, and the Holocaust rose in severity. Two days later, 26 Jews were executed in the Polish frontier town of Wieruszow. On September 4 of the same year, a thousand Jews were killed in one air raid over the Polish town of Sulejow, and 180 Jews were shot in the city of Czestochowa. On that same day, for refusing to burn the Torah, Rabbi Abraham Mordechai was burned alive. The mayhem continued, and on September 8 in Bedzin, Poland, 200 Jews sought refuge in their synagogue, which was then set on fire. On the same day, Jews in Germany were ordered to mark all businesses with a Star of David. On the 14th, the 1939 Jewish New Year, 43 Polish Jews were forced to do labor, then were shot to death. On the same day, Order No. 7 of German Civilian Administration transferred all Jewish industrial and commercial enterprises in Poland to Aryan hands. On the 21st, a conference was held in Berlin to discuss the long-term future of Jews, calling for ghettos to concentrate Jews in approved areas. And on September 23, the 1939 Rosh Hashanah, or Jewish Day of Atonement, Jews began to be persecuted with even greater severity by a new Nazi order. On the 28th, Germany and Russia partitioned Poland, with thousands of Jews removed, thousands more robbed, and hundreds murdered. All this during one month! And the terror that would become World War II was just beginning. [3]

- The Japanese made the decision to bombard Pearl Harbor, Hawaii—drawing the United States into World War II—in September of 1941. The actual bombing didn't take place until December 7, true, but the decision was made during the time leading up to the Day of Atonement.

- On Yom Kippur, the Day of Atonement and the holiest day in the 1973 Jewish calendar, Egypt and Syria opened a coordinated surprise attack against Israel. On the Golan Heights, approximately 180 Israeli tanks faced an onslaught of 1,400 Syrian tanks. Along the Suez Canal, fewer than 500 Israeli defenders were attacked by 80,000 Egyptians. Miraculously, Israeli forces, against insurmountable odds, drove the attackers back. Despite the Israel Defense Forces' ultimate success on the battlefield, a total of 2,688 soldiers were killed.[4]

- In more recent times, we have the example of the atrocious autumn tragedies taking place in New York City, Pennsylvania, and Washington, D.C., on September 11, 2001.

- Neither should it be surprising that more earthquakes occur in the three months of August, September, and October—revolving around the Day of Atonement— than in any other season of the year.

- Some memorable hurricanes have made their mark in the Atlantic and Gulf areas during September—Donna (1960), Carla (1961), Hugo (1989) and Georges (1998), to name a few. The deadliest (September 8, 1900—more than 6,000 died in Galveston, Texas) and the costliest (Katrina—August 29, 2005—$200 billion and counting) hurricanes in the history of the United States occurred during this season.

- Many of the worst and deadliest volcano eruptions in recorded history happened during this season, including Krakota, Indonesia (August 26–27, 1883—36,000 killed), Mount Vesuvius, Italy (August 24, AD 79—20,000 died), Mount Skaptar, Iceland (June–August, 1783—10,000 fatalities), Galunggung, Java (October 8 and 12, 1822—4,000 perished).

I could go on and on, but you can undoubtedly google better than I can. The big question is what? and when? and why?

More to the point, why would there be such a monumental, supernatural battle that rages throughout history during this one recurring, short season of the year?

There is obviously something unusual about this season. I don't claim to be a history expert, but I can connect dots, and I believe it should be obvious that Satan knows that the most important season of each year is the "latter" or time of Tabernacles, specifically the Day of Atonement. After years of Bible study, I also believe Satan knows that God declares special blessings for the next six months on people who honor His Day of Atonement!

Coincidence? I don't think so!

God established the feasts to be kept as consecrated, appointed holy times throughout both the Old and New Testaments. The blessings He offered (and still offers) are so great that we must step over man's traditions and observe, even celebrate, God's holy days. These are God's feasts. These are special days when God makes an appointment with each individual. If you show up and do what He says, the blessings are incredible!

Considering the spiritual and physical warfare waged over the Day of Atonement, the holiest day of the Jewish calendar, wouldn't it stand to reason that the greatest blessings are assigned to observance of that day and season?

It should make every believer overjoyed at the thought of what the Atonement blessings can bring!

SEASONS

Seasons are important to God. Often, for example, in both the Old and New Testaments, the former and latter seasons are mentioned. We know that in the latter season, God promises a double portion.

In Joel 2:23, the phrase "former rain" is used to mean spring, and the "latter rain" denotes the fall. Both rainy seasons, bookends for the hot Holy Land summers, are absolutely necessary for harvest. At the end of the spring rain came the grain harvest. After the autumn rains came the harvesting of fruit.

Spiritually, the former and latter rains correspond to the seven feast days given in Leviticus 23. The former season includes the first four feasts of Israel. The Passover season (Passover, Unleavened Bread, and Firstfruits) occurs during the spring of the year over a period of eight days. *Pentecost*—a word embodying the meaning "fifty"—occurs fifty days after Passover, and it has always been a time of great celebration and promise.

According to the Jewish calendar, the latter rain corresponds to the autumn Feast of Trumpets, Day of Atonement, and the Feast of Tabernacles. However, it is important to note that the Feast of Trumpets, or Rosh Hashanah, marks the Hebrew new year.

THE SEVEN BLESSINGS

Understanding the backdrop of the time surrounding the Tabernacles season and the Day of Atonement certainly puts the passage in Joel 2 in a completely new light, especially concerning the seven blessings of the Atonement that are given. After pointing to the "latter rain" fasting, weeping, and mourning (more about that later), Joel lists these specific blessings from the Lord related to this time:

> *Behold, I will send you grain and new wine and oil,*
> *And you will be satisfied by them;...*

> *Fear not, O land;*
> *Be glad and rejoice,*
> *For the LORD has done marvelous things! ...*
> *Rejoice in the LORD your God;*

[First Atonement Blessing: A Double Portion]

For He has given you the former rain faithfully,
And He will cause the rain to come down for you—
The former rain,
And the latter rain in the first month.

[Second Atonement Blessing: Financial Abundance]

The threshing floors shall be full of wheat,
And the vats shall overflow with new wine and oil.

[Third Atonement Blessing: Restoration]

So I will restore to you the years that the swarming locust has eaten,
The crawling locust,
The consuming locust,
And the chewing locust,
My great army which I sent among you.

[Fourth Atonement Blessing: Miracles]

You shall eat in plenty and be satisfied,
And praise the name of the LORD your God,
Who has dealt wondrously with you;
And My people shall never be put to shame.

[Fifth Atonement Blessing: God's Divine Presence]

Then you shall know that I am in the midst of Israel:
I am the LORD your God
And there is no other.
My people shall never be put to shame.

[Sixth Atonement Blessing: Blessings upon Your Family]

And it shall come to pass afterward

That I will pour out My Spirit on all flesh;

Your sons and your daughters shall prophesy,

Your old men shall dream dreams,

Your young men shall see visions.

And also on My menservants and on My maidservants

I will pour out My Spirit in those days.

And I will show wonders in the heavens and in the earth:

Blood and fire and pillars of smoke.

The sun shall be turned into darkness,

And the moon into blood,

Before the coming of the great and awesome day of the LORD.

[Seventh Atonement Blessing: Deliverance]

And it shall come to pass

That whoever calls on the name of the LORD

Shall be saved. (Joel 2:19, 21, 23-32)

The autumn season, specifically the time of Atonement, is a holy time with God. This was the time of which Joel was writing and prophesying.

The question is, are you ready for the seven blessings of the Atonement that are listed in Joel 2?

Very few Christians honor the Day of Atonement. God has given the Word to those of us who are beginning to understand and declare the significance of God's command to honor His holy days.

The trumpet has been sounded. The people of God everywhere are starting to catch the vision that God has put within the modern church: His holy days are still holy. His holy convocation is still being called to all who will listen.

Your Atonement Blessings Unleashed

It is interesting that before outlining the seven blessings listed in Joel 2, the Lord mentions the Day of Atonement instructions of fasting, weeping, and mourning, then gives us specific directions to bring an offering to the Lord:

> *"Now, therefore," says the* Lord,
> *"Turn to Me with all your heart,*
> *With fasting, with weeping, and with mourning."*
> *So rend your heart, and not your garments;*
> *Return to the* Lord *your God,*
> *For He is gracious and merciful,*
> *Slow to anger, and of great kindness;*
> *And He relents from doing harm.*
> *Who knows if He will turn and relent,*
> *And leave a blessing behind Him—*
> *A grain offering and a drink offering*
> *For the* Lord *your God?"* (Joel 2:12–14)

This should not be surprising to anyone who has spent much time in the Bible, for when God offers a covenant with His people, as He does with the seven blessings of the Atonement, it is a mutual obligation.

Deuteronomy 16:16-17 echoes other verses throughout the Scripture: *"And they shall not appear before the LORD empty-handed. Every man shall give as he is able, according to the blessing of the LORD your God which He has given you."*

The Bible is filled with cause-and-effect contracts: "If you do this, I will do this." Look at Luke 6:38, where our wonderful Lord declared, *"Give, and it will be given to you: good measure, pressed down, shaken together, and running over will be put into your bosom. For with the same measure that you use, it will be measured back to you."*

I am still discovering, for example, the amazing things that happen when obedient people unleash God's supernatural blessings through their "latter" season, Day of Atonement offering, It is literally Joel 2 in action!

So, what should you bring? First of all, we know that it is an offering during the Tabernacles or fall season, but it should be your tithe. It can be whatever God supplies. It should be sacrificial. It reflects your trust and faith in a God who stands ready to pour supernatural abundance upon your life.

The secret for all the Day of Atonement blessings, revealed individually in the next seven chapters, is very clear-cut: *"And they shall not appear before the LORD empty-handed"* (Deuteronomy 16:16).

Come with your special offering. Prove God. Then watch Him pour out more blessings than you can hold. Amazing things are just ahead! The Joel 2 blessings are just beginning for you.

Are you ready?

PART TWO

THE SEVEN ATONEMENT BLESSINGS

4

A DOUBLE PORTION

Rejoice in the LORD your God;
For He has given you the former rain faithfully,
And He will cause the rain to come down for you—
The former rain,
And the latter rain in the first month.

—JOEL 2:23

Before we discuss the first blessing of the Atonement—a double-portion economy God wants to pour over your life—let us back up a few verses in Joel 2 to get a perspective:

Blow the trumpet in Zion,
Consecrate a fast,
Call a sacred assembly;
Gather the people,
Sanctify the congregation,
Assemble the elders,

63

Gather the children and nursing babes;
Let the bridegroom go out from his chamber,
And the bride from her dressing room.
Let the priests, who minister to the LORD,
Weep between the porch and the altar;
Let them say, "Spare Your people, O LORD,
And do not give Your heritage to reproach,
That the nations should rule over them.
Why should they say among the peoples,
'Where is their God?'" (Joel 2:15-17)

We are given a powerful illustration of what happens when either a person or a nation follows God's prescribed plan. This happens during the latter, or Tabernacles, season. "Blow the trumpet in Zion" refers to the Feast of Trumpets, or Rosh Hashanah. Calling a time of fasting, weeping, and mourning refers to the Day of Atonement. In fact, earlier verses in the same chapter give an even more dramatic portrayal of what should happen in a person's (or nation's) heart as a prelude to what happens (figuratively and literally) in the time leading up to the rejoicing and divine harvest (Feast of Tabernacles), as well as the double-portion economy that happens after the Day of Atonement or Yom Kippur:

"Now, therefore," says the LORD,
"Turn to Me with all your heart,
With fasting, with weeping, and with mourning."
So rend your heart, and not your garments;
Return to the LORD your God,

For He is gracious and merciful,
Slow to anger, and of great kindness;
And He relents from doing harm.
Who knows if He will turn and relent,
And leave a blessing behind Him—
A grain offering and a drink offering
For the LORD your God? (Joel 2:12-14)

What a picture! We are told to prepare ourselves, to fast, to weep, to mourn, to rend our hearts (not the garments—God is interested more in what happens spiritually than all the outward ritual!), to return to the Lord, and to leave an offering.

What happens next defies human logic. It is a supernatural, double-portion economy!

Then the LORD will be zealous for His land,
And pity His people. The LORD will answer and say to His people,
"Behold, I will send you grain and new wine and oil,
And you will be satisfied by them;
I will no longer make you a reproach among the nations.
"But I will remove far from you the northern army,
And will drive him away into a barren and desolate land,
With his face toward the eastern sea
And his back toward the western sea;
His stench will come up,
And his foul odor will rise,
Because he has done monstrous things."

Fear not, O land;

Be glad and rejoice,

For the LORD *has done marvelous things!*

Do not be afraid, you beasts of the field;

For the open pastures are springing up,

And the tree bears its fruit;

The fig tree and the vine yield their strength.

Be glad then, you children of Zion,

And rejoice in the LORD *your God;*

For He has given you the former rain faithfully,

And He will cause the rain to come down for you—

The former rain,

And the latter rain in the first month. (Joel 2:18-23)

True Repentance

Yes, this passage of Scripture was written directly to Israel. But does that mean it only applies to Jews who lived in the Holy Land when God told Joel to pen these words?

Of course not! The Bible is timeless. It is given to people on a number of levels, some of which we understand now, and others which we will understand better as we *"grow in the grace and knowledge of our Lord and Savior Jesus Christ"* (2 Peter 3:18).

We are willing to claim the last part of Joel 2 as God's provision for His people today:

And it shall come to pass afterward

That I will pour out My Spirit on all flesh;

Your sons and your daughters shall prophesy,
Your old men shall dream dreams,
Your young men shall see visions.
And also on My menservants and on My maidservants
I will pour out My Spirit in those days.
And I will show wonders in the heavens and in the earth:
Blood and fire and pillars of smoke.
The sun shall be turned into darkness, And the moon into blood,
Before the coming of the great and awesome day of the LORD.
And it shall come to pass
That whoever calls on the name of the LORD
Shall be saved. (Joel 2:28-32)

What a description of the latter days! Something is getting ready to happen that has never happened. And as it gets darker and darker for the world, it will get brighter and brighter for believers who understand the times.

So if we quote these verses in faith, asking for God's divine provision and outpouring of the Holy Spirit, then why would we ever ignore the earlier part of the chapter—the seven blessings of the Atonement.

God wants to get your attention. He does that by calling you to repentance. He wants you to stop and see exactly where you are now—your deficiencies, your sins, your heart's condition. Before our Father can do all He wants to do, you must be prepared and ready.

A heart filled with the world's philosophy and the personal corruption that gathers there naturally is not a prepared place for God's double blessing.

Just as the Jews were told to do every year during the ten days leading up the Day of Atonement, it is time—continually—to seek God's face as never before.

There is no mystery here. The Bible is filled with verses to help us grasp the necessity and process of coming clean before the Lord: *"If My people who are called by My name will humble themselves, and pray and seek My face, and turn from their wicked ways, then I will hear from heaven, and will forgive their sin and heal their land"* (2 Chronicles 7:14).

Understandably, since the people of the Old Testament, to whom the passages were originally given, lived in an agriculturally based society, many of the word pictures are given which focus on farming:

- *"For thus says the LORD to the men of Judah and Jerusalem: 'Break up your fallow ground, and do not sow among thorns'"* (Jeremiah 4:3).

- *"Sow for yourselves righteousness; reap in mercy; break up your fallow ground, for it is time to seek the LORD, till He comes and rains righteousness on you"* (Hosea 10:12).

King David, after his greatest, most sinful defeat, finally realized how desperate his spiritual situation had become. In the midst of this realization, he penned these words (under the inspiration of the Holy Spirit), as a template for true repentance:

Behold, You desire truth in the inward parts,
And in the hidden part You will make me to know wisdom.
Purge me with hyssop, and I shall be clean;
Wash me, and I shall be whiter than snow.

Make me hear joy and gladness,
That the bones You have broken may rejoice.
Hide Your face from my sins,
And blot out all my iniquities.
Create in me a clean heart, O God,
And renew a steadfast spirit within me.
Do not cast me away from Your presence,
And do not take Your Holy Spirit from me.
Restore to me the joy of Your salvation,
And uphold me by Your generous Spirit.
Then I will teach transgressors Your ways,
And sinners shall be converted to You.
Deliver me from the guilt of bloodshed, O God,
The God of my salvation,
And my tongue shall sing aloud of Your righteousness.
O LORD, open my lips,
And my mouth shall show forth Your praise.
For You do not desire sacrifice, or else I would give it;
You do not delight in burnt offering.
The sacrifices of God are a broken spirit,
A broken and a contrite heart—
These, O God, You will not despise. (Psalm 51:6-17)

In the Old Testament, the two Hebrew verbs for *repentance* are *shuv* (to return) and *icham* (to feel sorrow). Throughout the Old Testament, *repentance* means confessing your sin to God, making a solemn promise to avoid committing the same sin again, and (as described in Leviticus 5) making prescribed offerings (which is why it is hardly strange that an offering is mentioned in Joel 2:14, just prior to the proclamation of the seven blessings of the Atonement).

In the New Testament, the Greek word for *repentance* is *metanoia* (a change of heart), and repentance is a central theme. When Jesus sent His followers out to preach the Gospel, He told them to call people to repentance (Mark 6:12; Luke 24:47). Teachings concerning repentance are found throughout the New Testament, especially in the writings of the apostles Peter (such as Acts 2:38) and Paul (Acts 20:21).

Repentance is more than an ethereal religious concept. It is the absolutely indispensable condition on which the salvation and redemption of the people of Israel, the church of God, as well as of every individual, depends.

Clearly, God wants everyone to repent: *"The Lord is not slack concerning His promise, as some count slackness, but is longsuffering toward us, not willing that any should perish but that all should come to repentance"* (2 Peter 3:9). Acts 17:30 tells us, *"Truly, these times of ignorance God overlooked, but now commands all men everywhere to repent."*

In fact, it is clear that failure on the part of anyone to heed God's call to repentance will result in eternal loss: *"I tell you, no; but unless you repent you will all likewise perish"* (Luke 13:3).

That said, understanding repentance isn't difficult; neither is doing it. It means more than just simply being sorry for something (most people spend a lifetime acknowledging that they mess up a lot). It actually must include an acknowledgment that we cannot make it by ourselves, we must return to God's plan, and we must be willing to change. As simple as that is, relatively few people practice true repentance because of those pesky ideas about following God's plan, not man's plan, and actually changing from what we want to do to what God desires for us.

As King David experienced, it isn't the outward ritual that makes a difference. It is a broken spirit, a contrite heart, a life opened and cleansed by the blood of the atoning Lamb of God.

Deuteronomy offers a powerful illustration of true repentance:

> *But from there you will seek the LORD your God, and you will find Him if you seek Him with all your heart and with all your soul. When you are in distress, and all these things come upon you in the latter days, when you turn to the LORD your God and obey His voice (for the LORD your God is a merciful God), He will not forsake you nor destroy you, nor forget the covenant of your fathers which He swore to them.* (Deuteronomy 4:29-31)

Take time now, and every day, to come clean. Practice your Day of Atonement often, not just once a year. You will be surprised at what God wants to do with the fertile ground of your heart that is plowed, prepared, planted, and ready for the former and latter rains to fall!

A New Economy

After calling His people to true repentance, God makes this promise as He refers to a supernatural economy based upon the double-blessing outpouring: *"Then the LORD will be zealous for His land, and pity His people. The LORD will answer and say to His people, 'Behold, I will send you grain and new wine and oil, and you will be satisfied by them; I will no longer make you a reproach among the nations'"* (Joel 2:18-19).

After pitying the people (giving mercy and forgiveness in direct response to true repentance), as the first blessing of the Atonement, God offers a powerful outpouring of the former and latter rain (more about that next).

But what is He blessing doubly? We have the threefold answer in verse 19:

- Grain (the core ingredient of the bread of life, meaning a fresh revelation of God's Word)

- Wine (a fresh anointing)

- Oil (symbolic of God's power)

In fact, not only will God give these three harvests, but after the double-blessing rains, your life will literally overflow with these blessings: *"The threshing floors shall be full of wheat, and the vats shall overflow with new wine and oil"* (Joel 2:24).

Full! Overflow! Is that something you want in your life?

I will discuss more about this full, overflowing abundance in the next chapter that focuses on finances. For the remainder of this chapter, however, I want to spotlight what God is doing on a deeper level to cause this overflow.

You see, the world has consistently scorned the church, but God says the day is coming soon when they will cease to mock. Why? We are getting ready to receive a supernatural overflow of the revelation of God's Word, a fresh anointing, and God's power!

Is it any wonder why God wants our hearts to be carefully and continually prepared. When He pours out the grain, wine, and oil upon our lives in massive supernatural proportions, everything will change.

Joel 2:21-22 tells us, *"Fear not, O land; be glad and rejoice, for the LORD has done marvelous things! Do not be afraid, you beasts of the field; for the open pastures are springing up, and the tree bears its fruit; the fig tree and the vine yield their strength."*

Something marvelous is about to happen that has never happened! The world will take notice. A new God-based economy, because of the double-portion season and not dependent upon shaky human precepts, is getting ready to take place.

Are you ready for this?

THE FORMER AND LATTER RAINS

Joel 2:23 speaks of something truly remarkable that will happen to those who move into the first blessing of the Atonement: *"Be glad then, you children of Zion, and rejoice in the LORD your God; for He has given you the former rain faithfully, and He will cause the rain to come down for you—the former rain, and the latter rain in the first month."*

What a prophecy—both rains together!

The Bible tells us that the first thing that will occur in our lives with the understanding of the Atonement is a double portion. But what does that mean?

The former rain deals with the spring rains and the latter rain deals with the fall rains. The first prepares the land for seed time and the latter prepares the land for harvest.

The "normal" economy in Joel's world was for the former rains to fall in the springtime in preparation for the grain harvests, and the latter rains to pour during the autumn in preparation for the fruit harvest.

What Joel prophesied, however, was the former and latter rain coming down in the first month of the Hebrew year—comparable to October or time of Atonement—and these rains would fall at the same time, a double blessing!

That is the harvest time happening before the seed time. Can you imagine a move of God so glorious that you will reap at the same time that you sow? There will be no time in-between waiting for the harvest to develop. That is exactly what the Lord said is going to happen.

That time is coming for believers who observe and tap into the fertile season that is quickly approaching.

A DIVINE DELUGE OF BLESSINGS

Are you beginning to understand what God is about to do? Everything about this outpouring will be supernatural. In this harvest we will see miracle after miracle.

Thus far we have only seen a mist, a sprinkle, a single rainfall. But the heavens are about to open wide and we will see a divine deluge of God's glory.

He declares, *"I will make them and the places all around My hill a blessing; and I will cause showers to come down in their season; there shall be showers of blessing"* (Ezekiel 34:26).

What are we commanded to do before the rain begins?

Get ready. Be prepared. Pray that the showers of harvest will begin falling now. God spoke through the prophet Zechariah, saying, *"Ask the LORD for rain in the time of the latter rain. The LORD will make flashing clouds; He will give them showers of rain, grass in the field for everyone"* (Zechariah 10:1).

The cloudburst that is about to be released is not determined by our schedule or human whims, but rather by the Father's plan. And I believe God has already appointed the time that is coming: *"They do not say in their heart, 'Let us now fear the LORD our God, who gives rain, both the former and the latter, in its season. He reserves for us the appointed weeks of the harvest"* (Jeremiah 5:24).

Again, the greatest barrier to receiving what God is preparing for us during this divine deluge is revealed in the following verse: *"Your iniquities have turned these things away, and your sins have withheld good from you"* (Jeremiah 5:25).

If you desire God's harvest on your life, leave evil and wickedness behind. Forget your foolish ways and seek the Lord until you find Him. Cry out to God, "Heal my life. Heal my home."

Let us seek God for this outpouring as never before. According to Scripture, here is what we can expect:

Come, and let us return to the LORD;
For He has torn, but He will heal us;
He has stricken, but He will bind us up.
After two days He will revive us;
On the third day He will raise us up,

That we may live in His sight.
Let us know,
Let us pursue the knowledge of the LORD.
His going forth is established as the morning;
He will come to us like the rain,
Like the latter and former rain to the earth. (Hosea 6:1-3)

Again and again, God tells us that the first and last rains are coming together! It won't be long.

THE DOUBLE-BLESSING ECONOMY

Notice that in God's first month, October, the stock market adjusts. For that matter, world economy adjusts at that time. The first and fourth quarters of the year are, in general, times when business does better. The second and third quarters of the year are moderate; the first and fourth quarters exceed.

The Word tells us that from March to October, God pours out His blessings moderately. During the latter season, God wants to pour out a double blessing. He is getting ready to do something spectacular.

What does this mean?

It means you need to get ready to be blessed far beyond anything you can imagine. God will cause affluence to come into your life, as you move into the blessings of the Atonement, in the form of nonwage prosperity. When God promises a double portion, it refers to something we obtain through position, not something we work to acquire! It means you will be overtaken, as God's Word promises, *"And all these blessings shall come upon you and overtake you, because you obey the voice of the LORD your God"* (Deuteronomy 28:2).

To this point, we have lived too long in the world's economy. We have embraced so little of what God has promised us. We must begin to think the way God wants us to think and receive His promises in our lives.

It's time to rise up! God's people are a mighty people. We must get the world's economy out of our minds. As a Christian, you can move into the Joel 2 economy. God's blessing is yours by promise.

DOUBLE-BLESSING FAITH

God desires to do marvelous things in your life. God's will is that you will never lack in any area of your life. He said, *"My people shall never be ashamed"* (Joel 2:26, KJV). I believe with all my heart that is exactly what God has promised His own.

It is up to us as His people to prepare our lives, to repent, to increasing our capacity to receive God's abiding and abundant grace. Isaiah speaks of this divine economy:

> *Enlarge the place of your tent,*
> *And let them stretch out the curtains of your dwellings;*
> *Do not spare;*
> *Lengthen your cords,*

And strengthen your stakes.
For you shall expand to the right and to the left,
And your descendants will inherit the nations,
And make the desolate cities inhabited.
Do not fear, for you will not be ashamed;
Neither be disgraced, for you will not be put to shame;
For you will forget the shame of your youth,
And will not remember the reproach of your widowhood anymore.
For your Maker is your husband,
The Lord of hosts is His name;
And your Redeemer is the Holy One of Israel;
He is called the God of the whole earth. (Isaiah 54:2-5)

Expanding to the right and the left! Not ashamed! Unafraid!

How would your life change if you truly began to receive the double blessing God is ready to pour out upon you?

It is time to embrace the double-blessing promises of God in your life. I love what Hebrews 11:13 says, *"These all died in faith, not having received the promises, but having seen them afar off, and were persuaded of them, and embraced them, and confessed that they were strangers and pilgrims on the earth."* You can actually take the Father's promises and press them close to your heart so they will never escape you.

You can see every promise God has made within your heart come to pass, for faith always has a destination. Faith is going somewhere and you are going there too when you put your whole heart into believing the precious promises in God's Word.

Deuteronomy 28:13 declares, *"And the LORD will make you the head and not the tail; you shall be above only, and not be beneath, if you heed the commandments of the LORD your God, which I command you today, and are careful to observe them."*

God's double-portion economy makes you the head, not the tail. It puts you above, not beneath. That is exactly the opposite of what the evil one wants to do in your life: *"The thief does not come except to steal, and to kill, and to destroy. I have come that they may have life, and that they may have it more abundantly"* (John 10:10).

Don't you know that Satan is just grinding his teeth at the thought that God's people will honor His holy Day of Atonement and receive His double-portion blessings? Don't you know that Satan knows the things that will come to us better than we know? Don't you know that he will do all in his power to deceive and discourage us from celebrating God's Atonement Day?

Tell him where to go—back home!

Lift your head and your heart and rejoice at the goodness of God. You are a member of the royal priesthood (1 Peter 2:9). You are part of the chosen latter-rain generation. You know your economy is dependent upon God, not man: *"You are of God, little children, and have overcome them, because He who is in you is greater than he who is in the world"* (1 John 4:4).

Isaiah 60:1 exhorts, *"Arise, shine; for your light has come! And the glory of the LORD is risen upon you."* You are no longer perishing for lack of knowledge. You are coming into a new revelation of God's timeless and imperishable Word.

God wants you to be the head, not the tail. You are to be above, not beneath. You are a person of victory, not defeat. You are called to live the double-portion life in God's economy, not man's!

You can arise today and claim your double-portion life. God wants to see you blessed in every area of your life. He intends for you to live abundantly today, anointed and highly favored!

Are you ready?

5

FINANCIAL ABUNDANCE

The threshing floors shall be full of wheat,
And the vats shall overflow with new wine and oil.

—JOEL 2:24

We could stop with the first blessing of the Atonement and be light years ahead of where so many people live today in man's economy. However, there are six more blessings outlined in Joel 2, and the next one, as part of God's supernatural economy, involves the promise of financial blessings and abundance.

I have mentioned this before, but in a day where fewer and fewer people live on farms, it is important to remember that Joel wrote these words, under the inspiration of the Holy Spirit, to people who mostly lived in an agrarian society. Therefore, he wrote in terms in which they were familiar.

If God were speaking through Joel today, we might be reading, "The factories will have plenty of orders, and you'll have to work overtime to fill the ones coming in." Or, "The offices will have so much work to do, they'll have to hire extra people to take care of the overflow."

God made this promise. It is not a lottery. It is not a smoke-and-mirrors sham. It is a sure thing for believers who understand that *"Heaven and earth will pass away, but My words will by no means pass away"* (Mark 13:31).

God's Blessings

As outlined in the previous chapter, blessings involve so much more than financial gain—grain (a fresh revelation of the Word of God, the bread of life), wine (a fresh anointing), and oil (a fresh overflow of God's power). Therefore, if your reason for succeeding and tapping into the Joel 2 blessings is merely to accumulate gold, silver, stock certificates, and real estate, I can tell you on the authority of God's Word that you will not triumph. Instead, you will reap pain and suffering. Scripture declares, *"He who trusts in his riches will fall, but the righteous will flourish like foliage"* (Proverbs 11:28).

Those who place their faith in finances may eventually lose both faith and finances. Their bank account may show a healthy balance, yet trouble is coming if a person's heart is empty and vain. *"He who loves silver will not be satisfied with silver; nor he who loves abundance, with increase. This also is vanity"* (Ecclesiastes 5:10).

However (and this is a big however!), God does promise financial abundance as the second blessing of the Atonement found in Joel 2:24. But it's also found throughout the Word.

To move into God's double-portion economy and to begin to claim financial abundance, you must begin to discover for yourself what the Word of God says. The Bible declares, *"My people are destroyed for lack of knowledge"* (Hosea 4:6).

Anyone who wants to gain a better understanding of true biblical prosperity has a treasury of proven guidelines provided throughout the Bible. You can grow into God's divine double-blessing economy by following His directions.

God Must Be Your Source

The worst mistake you can make in life—spiritually, emotionally, physically, and certainly financially—is to depend upon your own strength and knowledge. There is a place for self-reliance, of course, but you must put first things first.

Jesus did. There are 176 recorded instances throughout the four Gospels in which Jesus acknowledged His Father as His Source. My goodness, how can we do anything less?

You can make money through your own pull-yourself-up-by-your-bootstraps determination and human knowledge—there are plenty of examples of that throughout history and all around you, but only God can cause supernatural wealth to flow through you. Only He can teach you how to enter the realm of supernatural prosperity: *"Thus says the LORD, your Redeemer, the Holy One of Israel: "I am the LORD your God, who teaches you to profit, who leads you by the way you should go"* (Isaiah 48:17).

Your name may be on the title to your car or the deed to your house, but you are only holding the property in trust. It all belongs to God: *"The silver is Mine, and the gold is Mine, says the LORD of hosts"* (Haggai 2:8).

In reality, we are simply the caretakers of God's earthly possessions. These things are simply on loan to us by a Father who delights in the prosperity of His children! Never forget that it is God who grants us the ability to achieve, both spiritually and financially. That is why Moses stood before the children of Israel and said, *"And you shall remember the LORD your God, for it is He who gives you power to get wealth, that He may establish His covenant which He swore to your fathers, as it is this day"* (Deuteronomy 8:18).

You may have an MBA from a top business school, and you may own more than anyone around you, but your education is not complete until you sit at the feet of the Master Teacher. Listen to what He announced through His prophet Isaiah: *"Thus says the LORD, your Redeemer, the Holy One of Israel: "I am the LORD your God, who teaches you to profit, who leads you by the way you should go"* (Isaiah 48:17).

If you want your assets to exceed your liabilities, learn your double-portion accounting from the Almighty, the One who "teaches you to profit." It all begins by acknowledging Him as your Source.

BE OBEDIENT TO GOD THROUGH YOUR FINANCES

The release of God's blessings in your life is directly connected to your obedience. In fact, obedience to God's Word is vital to your financial success, for the Bible declares: *"This Book of the Law shall not depart from your mouth, but you shall meditate in it day and night, that you may observe to do according to all that is written in it. For then you will make your way prosperous, and then you will have good success"* (Joshua 1:8).

This is also why we are told in Deuteronomy 28:2: *"And all these blessings shall come upon you and overtake you, because you obey the voice of the Lord your God."*

Prosperity isn't the result of pursuing wealth; it comes from obedience. And what a marvelous exchange it is. If we obey the covenants of God, He will *"open for you the windows of heaven and pour out for you such blessing that there will not be room enough to receive it"* (Malachi 3:10).

There are so many examples of this financial blessing due to obedience throughout Scripture that book after book has been written on the subject.

Look in 2 Chronicles 26, for example. You don't hear many sermons on this relatively obscure lad who was named king of Judah when he was only sixteen. However, it is interesting to note, in the midst of this portion of Scripture, God thought it was important to tell us these words: *"And he did what was right in the sight of the Lord, according to all that his father Amaziah had done. He sought God in the days of Zechariah, who had understanding in the visions of God; and as long as he sought the Lord, God made him prosper"* (2 Chronicles 26:4-5).

When did he flourish and grow? "As long as he sought the Lord." Even more, God *made* him prosper.

Do you realize that if you obey God's commands and seek His face, failure is not an option? The Lord makes certain that you succeed, and in His double-portion economy, even your mistakes will be transformed into blessing.

I rejoice every time I read in the first Psalm:

Blessed is the man
Who walks not in the counsel of the ungodly,
Nor stands in the path of sinners,
Nor sits in the seat of the scornful;
But his delight is in the law of the LORD,
And in His law he meditates day and night.
He shall be like a tree planted by the rivers of water,
That brings forth its fruit in its season,
Whose leaf also shall not wither;
And whatever he does shall prosper. (Psalm 1:1-3)

When you are obedient, the Lord will pour out wisdom and understanding of how to prosper: *"Only may the* LORD *give you wisdom and understanding, and give you charge concerning Israel, that you may keep the law of the* LORD *your God. Then you will prosper, if you take care to fulfill the statutes and judgments with which the* LORD *charged Moses concerning Israel. Be strong and of good courage; do not fear nor be dismayed"* (1 Chronicles 22:12-13).

Proverbs 9:10 tells us, *"The fear of the* LORD *is the beginning of wisdom, and the knowledge of the Holy One is understanding."* Similarly, Proverbs 1:7 declares, *"The fear of the* LORD *is the beginning of knowledge, but fools despise wisdom and instruction."*

God desires to teach you supernaturally about His double-portion economy about the things you could not know in the natural: *"Thus says the* LORD, *your Redeemer, the Holy One of Israel: "I am the* LORD *your God, who teaches you to profit, who leads you by the way you should go"* (Isaiah 48:17).

The Bible, as I've written before, is absolutely chockfull of promises of

"If you do this, God will do that." It all comes down to obedience. Stop fearing the laws of the Lord. Delight in such passages as Deuteronomy 28. Meditate day and night on treasured scriptures such as Psalm 112. Be obedient to God, and whatever you do will prosper.

BE DILIGENT

We've all heard the old saying, "Work as if it all depends on you, and pray as if it all depends on God." The truth is that everything depends on God, our Source, but He also expects us to be diligent in order to tap into the financial blessings of His double-portion economy.

There are instructions throughout the Bible about the benefits of working diligently, including this one from Proverbs 10:4-5: *"He who has a slack hand becomes poor, but the hand of the diligent makes rich. He who gathers in summer is a wise son; he who sleeps in harvest is a son who causes shame."*

Working should never be an end in itself, for total dependence upon the world's economic system will leave you lacking. Working enables you to give, but giving is what causes you to prosper, though, by the planting of your seed in anointed ground, as we are told in Ephesians 4:28: *"Let him who stole steal no longer, but rather let him labor, working with his hands what is good, that he may have something to give him who has need."*

BE A GIVER

Begin by giving your tithe and offerings to God: *"Bring all the tithes into the storehouse, that there may be food in My house, and try Me now in this, says the* LORD *of hosts, if I will not open for you the windows of heaven and pour out for you such blessing that there will not be room enough to receive it"* (Malachi 3:10).

Not room enough to receive it! Those are pretty good cause-and-effect benefits, don't you think?

The tithe is a tenth of your income, no more and no less. So you don't really "give" your tithe, since it is already His. You acknowledge His ownership of everything you possess through your tithe. Whatever you give above the tithe is your offering, which is what moves you into supernatural "more than enough" prosperity. This foundation is basic and unchangeable. Without it, the blessings from any offering—Atonement or otherwise—will not be effective.

And as a giver, it is important to realize that when the double-blessing rains fall, how do you reap a double harvest? You do so by planting twice as many seeds, right?

Here is the secret of the double blessing. Give. Do something unusual. God offers a key to unlock the doors to power and wisdom, to abundance, debt-free living, and to a strong family heritage.

Does that sound too good to be true?

The key is giving. It is not a gimmick. It is not the latest fad. It is simply God's principle that has worked since the beginning of time.

Today, many of the top corporate executives I have met understand this principle, even those who aren't grounded in the Word. They are generally givers. The same goes for the best political leaders and high achievers. Success and giving go hand in hand.

The true secret, however, isn't just giving. It is giving according to God's plan. Giving gives God glory, for every time you offer praise or tangible gifts, you give God glory. The Bible is filled with accounts of people who brought what they had in their hands—large or small—and were blessed with overwhelming abundance. It is a breakthrough moment when you finally realize what a giving heart does for your spiritual life. Giving brings openness to whatever God decides to do in an area of your life!

Giving enables you to come into God's presence properly. Abraham understood this, according to Genesis 14, for he gave an offering to Melchizedek. This was four hundred years before the law was given to Moses, yet Abraham knew then what believers need to know today. To receive blessings from being in God's presence, you must come with an open, giving heart. The offering is tangible evidence of your inner desire. As we see in the Old Testament, a giving heart builds a powerful legacy that moved from generation to generation, extending from Abraham to Isaac, Jacob and beyond. There are certain steps to coming into God's courts. Giving enables you to do it properly.

I have seen these principles proven in my own life over and over. Those times when you are tempted to look upon giving as a mere exercise or something you have to do, the results are always less than satisfactory. But I have found that when I give with an open, fresh heart, I always receive accordingly.

GIVE TO HELP OTHERS

Why does the Lord want you to prosper? Is it to increase the spending limit on your VISA or MasterCard? Is it to provide collateral for a larger mortgage?

No!

I am fully convinced that God wants to bestow financial blessing on people who will generously support His work and help carry the message of His Son to the world.

Proverbs 28:27 even tells us that we are to give to people in situations where there is no human hope of financial return: *"He who gives to the poor will not lack, but he who hides his eyes will have many curses."* How extreme is that?

Do you want to have a life with no lack? Be a giver! Make it a way of life. Get so good at it that you are actually happier to give than to receive: *"But this I say: He who sows sparingly will also reap sparingly, and he who sows bountifully will also reap bountifully. So let each one give as he purposes in his heart, not grudgingly or of necessity; for God loves a cheerful giver"* (2 Corinthians 9:6-7).

God will pour out His abundant blessings on you when you give cheerfully to others from a generous heart!

GET RADICAL IN YOUR GIVING

One definition of insanity is doing the same old thing, again and again, but expecting different results. If what you have been doing in the past isn't working, why not do something different?

Get radical!

It's what the widow with two mites did. She gave sacrificially, and Jesus Christ thought it was such a powerful act of faith that He pointed to her gift then, and it has been repeated through the ages to readers of the New Testament: *"So He called His disciples to Himself and said to them, 'Assuredly, I say to you that this poor widow has put in more than all those who have given to the treasury; for they all put in out of their abundance, but she out of her poverty put in all that she had, her whole livelihood'"* (Mark 12:43-44).

It's what the widow from Zarephath did (1 Kings 17). She got extremely radical by stepping out in faith and giving the prophet Elijah her last meal. What happened to her was beyond any natural harvest: *"The bin of flour was not used up, nor did the jar of oil run dry, according to the word of the LORD which He spoke by Elijah"* (verse 16).

It is time that we begin to do the unusual for our glorious Lord and King, for He does not respond to the usual. He only responds to the unusual. It is time we step out and start giving radically, for extreme days are here. God is looking for a people who will do the unusual with Him and for Him!

GIVE RADICALLY TO DEFEAT SATAN'S PLAN FOR YOUR LIFE

Did you know that as you become an extreme giver and as you tap into God's double-portion economy, you also make the evil one gnash his teeth?

Seriously! It's actually in the Bible.

In Psalm 112, the psalmist begins by presenting the requirements for experiencing God's financial blessing and the benefits:

Praise the LORD!
Blessed is the man who fears the LORD,
Who delights greatly in His commandments.

His descendants will be mighty on earth;
The generation of the upright will be blessed.
Wealth and riches will be in his house,
And his righteousness endures forever.
Unto the upright there arises light in the darkness;
He is gracious, and full of compassion, and righteous.
A good man deals graciously and lends;
He will guide his affairs with discretion.
Surely he will never be shaken;
The righteous will be in everlasting remembrance.
He will not be afraid of evil tidings;
His heart is steadfast, trusting in the LORD.
His heart is established;
He will not be afraid,
Until he sees his desire upon his enemies.
He has dispersed abroad,
He has given to the poor;
His righteousness endures forever;
His horn will be exalted with honor. (Psalm 112:1-9)

What a magnificent promise for the person who builds his future on God's principles. Yet there is more! The scripture then paints a vivid picture of what happens when "the wicked"—including Satan and his followers—come face to face with such biblical prosperity.

The next verse, Psalm 112:10, declares, *"The wicked will see it and be grieved; he will gnash his teeth and melt away; the desire of the wicked shall perish."*

When Satan sees that you are blessed, it torments him. It makes him grind his teeth. It even makes him melt away in retreat.

Become a radical giver as you tap into God's economy, if for no other reason than to chase Satan from your life!

GIVE YOUR ATONEMENT OFFERING

I have mentioned this before, and since this book focuses on the blessings of the Atonement, it is important to highlight the verse in Joel 2:14, just before all seven blessings are promised: *"And leave a blessing behind Him—a grain offering and a drink offering for the LORD your God?"*

Notice in the Exodus 23 passage that outlines all the feasts, God says, *"None shall appear before Me empty"* (verse 15).

Get radical with your Atonement offering! If you want a double-portion life, start giving in a double-portion manner. If you want to experience God's boundless provision to *"supply all your need according to his riches in glory by Christ Jesus"* (Philippians 4:19), then start giving boundlessly. If you want no lack, *"always having all sufficiency in all things"* (2 Corinthians 9:8), then become an extreme giver.

You don't know how?

God is ready to teach you how to give, how to profit, and how to establish a powerful heritage of giving in your family. So if you want to see increase in your finances, what are you willing to do? Are you willing to do something out of the ordinary? Are you willing to get radical in your giving? The Word of God tells us that the God we serve is moved when He sees His children do the unusual in faith.

It is time that you understand the double blessing. It is time to understand the great keys of success that will allow you to participate freely in the great outpouring that is starting to be poured out during the latter season.

It is time to unleash Isaiah 48:17 in your life: *"Thus saith the LORD, thy Redeemer, the Holy One of Israel, I am the LORD thy God which teacheth thee to profit, which leadeth thee by the way that thou shouldest go"* (KJV).

GET EXCITED NOW FOR THE OUTPOURING TO COME

Farmers understand this. Even as they cultivate the soil and plant the tiny seeds, and even as they see the first hint of green coming out of the ground, there is always a growing excitement at what God is preparing to do.

Your coming double-portion blessing is worth getting excited about. The Bible says, *"Let them shout for joy and be glad, who favor my righteous cause; and let them say continually, 'Let the LORD be magnified, who has pleasure in the prosperity of His servant'"* (Psalm 35:27).

To the children of Israel Moses declared:

> *The LORD your God will make you abound in all the work of your hand, in the fruit of your body, in the increase of your livestock, and in the produce of your land for good. For the LORD will again rejoice over you for good as He rejoiced over your fathers, if you obey the voice of the LORD your God, to keep His commandments and His statutes which*

are written in this Book of the Law, and if you turn to the
Lord your God with all your heart and with all your soul.
(Deuteronomy 30:9-10)

Then Moses added these important words, *"Now what I am commanding you today is not too difficult for you or beyond your reach"* (Deuteronomy 30:11, NIV)

This is possible! It is not pie-in-the-sky. In fact, why should anything be impossible when the Lord is your partner?

And if He delights in your prosperity, why shouldn't you get excited, too! Go ahead, rejoice in the fact that all of His resources are yours!

KINGDOM PROSPERITY

God actually desires for you to prosper: *"Beloved, I pray that you may prosper in all things and be in health, just as your soul prospers"* (3 John 2). As your soul grows and prospers, so will the rest of you. As you study the Word and apply its principles, God will give you greater prosperity.

As a result, *"the threshing floors shall be full of wheat, and the vats shall overflow with new wine and oil"* (Joel 2:24). This second blessing of the Atonement will cause overflow.

God wants to bless you in every area of your life, including your finances. There is no limit to God's supply, for His resources are inexhaustible: *"And my God shall supply all your need according to His riches in glory by Christ Jesus"* (Philippians 4:19).

God has a wonderful plan for your financial future. The Bible is filled with promises of the Father's blessings for those who understand and obey the Creator's fixed laws of sowing and reaping, especially when believers also realize the importance of the Atonement offering. As you apply His kingdom principles, you can live an abundant life filled with financial miracles!

What seeds are you willing to plant in order to reap a bountiful, supernatural, double-portion harvest of Atonement blessings?

Get radical in your giving!

6
RESTORATION

So I will restore to you the years that the swarming locust has eaten,
The crawling locust,
The consuming locust,
And the chewing locust.

—JOEL 2:25

The first Atonement blessing was a supernatural, double-portion economy. The second involved an overflow of financial blessings. The third, for those who honor His Day of Atonement, is restoration.

God promised that He will give back to you whatever the devil has taken away from you. Whatever you have lost, it is time for recovery and restoration.

SUPERNATURAL RESTORATION

God has promised you restoration. It is not something for which you must merely hope. It is a promise of God.

But what does it mean?

How would you like to regain all that has been taken, stolen, and lost?

How would you like to regain your strength as your are restored to health, rescued from destruction, established in God's kingdom, and made new?

How would you like to have your lost time redeemed as you are refreshed, replenished, revived, and recover all?

Restoration is the third supernatural blessing of the Atonement. This isn't something I'm making up—Joel 2:25 is very clear!

In fact, the entire Bible—from Genesis to Revelation—is the story of God's restoration. God created man and woman and placed them in an abundant, marvelous garden where they had all that they could ever want or need, yet they fell away from the Lord. Adam and Eve lost all. Then the restoration process began. Eventually, Jesus Christ came to recover what was lost, once and for all. In the end, the fulfillment of the victory on the cross will be complete! In between, the Bible contains example after example of divine restoration.

JOB RESTORED

Nothing is lost when you serve God. The Lord Jesus promised, *"And everyone who has left houses or brothers or sisters or father or mother or wife or children or lands, for My name's sake, shall receive a hundredfold, and inherit eternal life"* (Matthew 19:29). God will command His blessings upon you when your commitment to Him is steadfast and true.

God said that if you serve Him, *"So you shall serve the LORD your God, and He will bless your bread and your water. And I will take sickness away from the midst of you"* (Exodus 23:25). As you abide in Christ, God will multiply everything you touch, keep your children safe, watch over your home, and drive the enemy away from you.

Think about Job, for example, who thought that he lost everything, yet he recovered all. Even though Job was at his lowest point, he prayed, *"I know that You can do everything, and that no purpose of Yours can be withheld from You"* (Job 42:2).

As a result, Job's trust in the Lord remained strong and true despite his circumstances. The Lord was pleased with Job, and nothing was lost by him: *"And the LORD restored Job's losses when he prayed for his friends. Indeed the LORD gave Job twice as much as he had before"* (Job 42:10).

The Word of God goes on to say, *"Now the LORD blessed the latter days of Job more than his beginning"* (Job 42:12). What looked like a loss in Job's life really was not a loss at all. In fact, because Job trusted in the Lord, God gave him more in the end than he had in the beginning.

KING DAVID RESTORED

The account of a ragtag band of soldiers, as recorded in 1 Samuel 22 through 30, must surely be one of the most amazing restoration victories of any group in history.[1]

David, already anointed by the prophet Samuel to be the next king of Israel, and already a celebrated hero for his victory over the giant Goliath, suddenly had to flee for his life because of King Saul's jealousy.

David, warned by Jonathan, Saul's son, ended up hiding in a cave. It must have been a rather large cavern, for he was soon joined by a strange band of four hundred troubled followers:

*David therefore departed from there and escaped to the cave
of Adullam. And when his brothers and all his father's house
heard it, they went down there to him. And everyone who
was in distress, everyone who was in debt, and everyone who
was discontented gathered to him. So he became captain
over them. And there were about four hundred men with
him.* (1 Samuel 22:1-2)

Pastor Benny Hinn, in his book *Total Recovery*, calls the group
"the original 3-D army," since they were overcome with distress,
debt, and discontent. It's the perfect description of the group housed
in Adullam's dank cave.

God was there when David faced wild animals as a shepherd boy.
He was there when a youthful David stood in Goliath's massive shadow.
He was there when David hid from Saul in the cave. God was there as
David began leading his band of soldiers away from the troubles. From
what we read throughout Psalms, he was a champion encourager.

By 1 Samuel 30, when Ziklag and the Amalekites invaded the
land and took their families captive, the army had changed. When
God gave David and the men the go-ahead, they pursued the enemy,
rescued their families, and took the spoils of battle.

Three words written in that chapter, *"David recovered all"* (verse
19), are filled with meaning. Not only did it reveal God's power of
restoration, but it began a virtually unbroken chain of victories and
prosperity for David.

What happened between the accounts recorded in 1 Samuel 20

and 30 to make such a difference? Whatever it was, David came to
the place where he could write:

> The LORD is my shepherd;
> I shall not want.
> He makes me to lie down in green pastures;
> He leads me beside the still waters.
> He restores my soul;
> He leads me in the paths of righteousness
> For His name's sake.
>
> Yea, though I walk through the valley of the shadow of death,
> I will fear no evil;
> For You are with me;
> Your rod and Your staff, they comfort me.
>
> You prepare a table before me in the presence of my enemies;
> You anoint my head with oil;
> My cup runs over.
> Surely goodness and mercy shall follow me
> All the days of my life;
> And I will dwell in the house of the LORD Forever. (Psalm 23)

God restored David! And within a single generation, the country
was literally teeming with abundance and plenty for everyone.
According to 2 Chronicles 1:15, by the time Solomon became king

of Israel, silver and gold were as plenteous as stones: *"Also the king made silver and gold as common in Jerusalem as stones, and he made cedars as abundant as the sycamores which are in the lowland."* Can you imagine? That's restoration and more. God used David to build a powerful, victorious nation out of a small band of people who had once been mired in distress, debt, and discouragement.

David knew precisely what God was capable of doing when he penned these words: *"Call upon Me in the day of trouble; I will deliver you, and you shall glorify Me"* (Psalm 50:15).

God wants to be there with you in the midst of your times of trouble, as well. During those moments, you can call upon the Lord. Your Redeemer, Christ Jesus, is standing by to help when distress, worry, grief, affliction, pain, depression, entanglement, setbacks, sorrow, and loss come to your life. God hears the cry of those who are in trouble, and He desires to restore all!

The Prodigal Son Restored

The prodigal son is another example of a man who lost everything due to his own mistakes, yet he recovered all when he returned to his father. There came a point in the prodigal son's life where he realized the mistake that he made. The Bible says the prodigal son *"came to himself"* and asked, *"how many hired servants of my father's have bread enough and to spare, and I perish with hunger!"* (Luke 15:17). He decided that he would return to his father and repent for what he had done.

Luke recounts this parable, picking up the narrative when the prodigal son finally decided to go back home and ask forgiveness:

I will arise and go to my father, and will say to him, "Father, I have sinned against heaven and before you, and I am no longer worthy to be called your son. Make me like one of your hired servants." And he arose and came to his father. But when he was still a great way off, his father saw him and had compassion, and ran and fell on his neck and kissed him. And the son said to him, "Father, I have sinned against heaven and in your sight, and am no longer worthy to be called your son." But the father said to his servants, "Bring out the best robe and put it on him, and put a ring on his hand and sandals on his feet. And bring the fatted calf here and kill it, and let us eat and be merry; for this my son was dead and is alive again; he was lost and is found." And they began to be merry. (Luke 15:18-24)

Restored!

Just like the prodigal son, think about how much you have lost in the past, perhaps through your own doing. You may have believed that what you lost was gone forever. That is not true. God desires to restore all!

THE APOSTLE PETER RESTORED

You might wonder about some of the things that you have lost, saying, "It was my own fault that I lost them. I understand that the Lord will restore what the thief has stolen, but I lost some things in my life due to my own sin."

We see an example of restoration in the life of Peter the apostle. It was Peter's decision to deny Christ. He cursed and said that he did not know the Lord Jesus. Yet less than a hundred days later, he preached on the Day of Pentecost and about three thousand people were born again (Acts 2:41).

Yes, Peter denied the Lord, but he was still anointed of God and preached with power!

Charles H. Spurgeon spoke many times about Peter's restoration, including this memorable sermon at the Metropolitan Tabernacle:

> Peter was never ashamed after this. Who was it that stood up at Pentecost and preached? Was it not Peter? Was he not always foremost in testifying to his Lord and Master? I trust that if any of us have been falling back, and especially if we have wandered into sin, we may get such a restoration from the Lord himself, that we may become better Christians ever afterwards. I do not want you to break a bone, I pray God you never may; but if you ever do, may the heavenly Surgeon so set it that it may become thicker and stronger than before. Courage was the bone in Peter which snapped; but when it was set, it became the strongest bone in his nature, and never broke again. When the Lord sets the bones of his people, they never break any more—he does his work so effectually. The man who has erred by anger becomes meek and gentle. The man who has erred by drink quits the deadly cup, and loathes it. The man who has sinned by shame becomes the bravest of the company. [2]

God could have said, "You made a mistake, Peter, and for that you've disqualified yourself from ever being used by Me."

However, that is not what the Lord said to Peter, and that is not what God says to you. Instead of condemning Peter, God anointed him and said, *"Feed my sheep."*

The Bible makes it clear that God keeps no record of wrongs. Psalm 103:10-12 says, *"He has not dealt with us according to our sins, nor punished us according to our iniquities. For as the heavens are high above the earth, so great is His mercy toward those who fear Him; as far as the east is from the west, so far has He removed our transgressions from us."*

Jesus did not change His mind about Peter when Peter made a mistake, and the Lord has not changed His mind about you over your mistakes. Like the prodigal son or Peter, all you must do is return to your heavenly Father. God will bring total restoration to you, even when it is your own fault that you have experienced loss.

Your Restoration

Your own life is also a story of recovery. Once you were lost, and now you are found. Once you were blind, and now you can see. The second you were born again, you came under the law of resurrection and you were delivered from the law of destruction.

The Lord has already performed the promises in His Word for you. So why should restoration be a foreign thing to you? God's love is so great for you that He has been leading you toward total recovery, even while you did not know how much you needed to be rescued from sin and destruction.

In God's great mercy, He brought you out of darkness and into light, out of sickness and into health, out of bondage and into liberty.

Ever since the day that you became a Christian, the power of God has been working in you to reverse what the devil has stolen. Through Christ, we go from death to life. Romans 8:2 says, *"For the law of the Spirit of life in Christ Jesus has made me free from the law of sin and death."* As believers, we operate under a different law than the world does.

When Jesus entered your life, God said you would now go from darkness to light, sickness to health, bondage to liberty, and weakness to strength. Psalm 30:11 says, *"You have turned for me my mourning into dancing; you have put off my sackcloth and clothed me with gladness."*

Your Legal Right

Supernatural restoration is a process that begins in our Savior. As your life is filled with God's Word, and you act upon your faith, you will have the authority to take back or regain what has been stolen from you. It is your legal right to reclaim what belongs to you.

The law of God concerning a thief is clear in the Bible, and the Word tells us that Satan is a thief. Therefore, the law of God applies to him regarding what has been stolen from you. Exodus 22:7 says that when anything is *"stolen out of the man's house, if the thief is found, he shall pay double."*

The devil has stolen from you. He is a thief who comes to *"steal, and to kill, and to destroy"* (John 10:10). The devil must make full restitution for what he has stolen from you. That is the law of God, and the devil must obey it.

It is time you subpoena the devil, in the name of Jesus, and bring an indictment against him, find him guilty, and force him to restore double. Our God is the God of the lost and found. This is your day to find and recover what you have lost!

RESTORATION THEN AND NOW

One day in heaven, we will experience the complete fullness of God, but it is important not overlook that God wants you to be blessed here on earth right now. The Lord's will is to see you whole, your life restored, and all that you have lost totally recovered.

Charles H. Spurgeon, the powerful Bible teacher, taught about the process of restoration:

> It will strike you at once that the locusts did not eat the years: the locusts ate the fruits of the years' labor, the harvests of the fields; so that the meaning of the restoration of the years must be the restoration of those fruits and of those harvests which the locusts consumed. You cannot have back your time; but there is a strange and wonderful way in which God can give back to you the wasted blessings, the unripened fruits of years over which you mourned. The fruits of wasted years may yet be yours. It is a pity that they should have been eaten by

your folly and negligence. But if they have been so, be not hopeless concerning them. "All things are possible to him that believes." There is a power which is beyond all things and can work great marvels.[3]

Forget about what happened yesterday. Bury the past. God urges: *"Do not remember the former things, nor consider the things of old. Behold, I will do a new thing, now it shall spring forth; shall you not know it? I will even make a road in the wilderness and rivers in the desert"* (Isaiah 43:18-19).

As in salvation, *"Therefore, if anyone is in Christ, he is a new creation; old things have passed away; behold, all things have become new"* (2 Corinthians 5:17).

Clear your mind of yesterday's misery, pain, confusion, and sorrow. Focus on tomorrow in the mighty name of Jesus and you will be restored. God has promised it as one of the seven blessings of the Atonement.

Now, claim your restoration!

7

MIRACLES

You shall eat in plenty and be satisfied,
And praise the name of the LORD your God,
Who has dealt wondrously with you;
And My people shall never be put to shame.

—JOEL 2:26

As the fourth blessing of the Atonement, God promises not only that you will have plenty and be satisfied, but also that our Father will deal wondrously with you.

Wondrously—as in performing wonders!

God has always performed signs and wonders on behalf of His people, starting with what He did in Genesis 1.

We know what He did to rescue Israel from captivity: *"You have brought Your people Israel out of the land of Egypt with signs and wonders, with a strong hand and an outstretched arm, and with great terror"* (Jeremiah 32:21).

Daniel wrote, *"How great are His signs, and how mighty His wonders! His kingdom is an everlasting kingdom, and His dominion is from generation to generation"* (Daniel 4:3). He saw some pretty impressive miracles up close, including his salvation from the lion's den, so he knew firsthand, *"He delivers and rescues, and He works signs and wonders in heaven and on earth, who has delivered Daniel from the power of the lions"* (Daniel 6:27).

Jesus Christ was known far and wide during His earthly ministry for the miraculous that happened everywhere He went: *"Men of Israel, hear these words: Jesus of Nazareth, a Man attested by God to you by miracles, wonders, and signs which God did through Him in your midst, as you yourselves also know"* (Acts 2:22).

Just before ascending into heaven, Jesus spoke clearly concerning the need for the miraculous in the spreading of the Gospel:

> *And he said unto them, Go ye into all the world, and preach the gospel to every creature. He that believeth and is baptized shall be saved; but he that believeth not shall be damned. And these signs shall follow them that believe; In my name shall they cast out devils; they shall speak with new tongues; They shall take up serpents; and if they drink any deadly thing, it shall not hurt them; they shall lay hands on the sick, and they shall recover.* (Mark 16:15-18, KJV)

His followers were also known from that point by the miracles that God performed in their midst: *"And through the hands of the apostles many signs and wonders were done among the people"* (Acts 5:12).

Throughout history, God has clearly shown Himself through the miraculous: *"God also bearing witness both with signs and wonders, with various miracles, and gifts of the Holy Spirit, according to His own will"* (Hebrews 2:4).

God desires to pour out the miraculous. Joel 2's description of dealing "wondrously" reveals the fact that He will do things for you that your eyes have never before seen. You will hear things you have never heard before. He will bring about things you cannot even imagine. That is dealing wondrously with you.

Are you ready for this?

Are you ready for wonders, signs, and so many incredible things?

It is what will happen when you honor His Word and His holy day.

THE MIRACULOUS

According to the dictionary, a miracle is an event that appears to be contrary to the laws of nature and is regarded as an act of God; an event or action that is totally amazing, extraordinary, or unexpected.

Most believers in the world today, regardless of their denominational background, generally acknowledge that God has the power to perform miracles. However, their views on how and when He shows Himself through signs and wonders present a variety of opinions.

Rather than talking about the broad subject of miracles, let's focus on miracles of divine intervention and healing.

Some hold firmly to the belief that God does not do these things today, maintaining that He did heal in what they refer to as "the day of miracles," a time when Jesus was on earth. People who believe this way assert with deep conviction that since Jesus is no longer on earth physically to perform supernatural works, miracles are no longer possible.

Others admit reluctantly that God, at times, may still heal some needy individual, rescuing that person from certain tragedy through an act of divine intervention. There are also those who advocate a "mind over matter" approach, insisting that by maintaining a strong mental attitude, victory can be realized over sickness and adversity.

Mankind has many theories about God, of course, and the question of miracles has been discussed and debated for centuries by some of the greatest theologians. Yet man's ideas have no bearing on God Almighty. The Bible is the final authority on healing and miracles, and only through its sacred pages can we discover the true nature and character of God, along with the benefits and blessings that belong to us as His children.

What Does the Bible Tell Us?

Let's talk even more specifically about divine healing. The Scriptures tell us clearly that it is God's will to heal His children today and that it is His desire for us to enjoy the blessings of divine health and His healing touch. Both the Old and New Testaments have much to say about miracles of healing.

God's ever-present disposition toward us regarding health and healing is revealed in His covenant of healing with the children of

Israel: *"If you diligently heed the voice of the* LORD *your God and do what is right in His sight, give ear to His commandments and keep all His statutes, I will put none of the diseases on you which I have brought on the Egyptians. For I am the* LORD *who heals you"* (Exodus 15:26). He said *I am* the God—in present tense. He didn't say *I was,* not I *will be,* but *I am*!

God is ever-present. We are told, *"Jesus Christ is the same yesterday, today, and forever"* (Hebrews 13:8). There are no boundaries, limitations, or time constraints on God's promises. His promise to us for healing and health is the same today as it was to any past generation.

The words of David acknowledged that covenant when he said, *"Bless the* LORD*, O my soul; and all that is within me, bless His holy name! Bless the* LORD*, O my soul, and forget not all His benefits: who forgives all your iniquities, who heals all your diseases"* (Psalm 103:1-3).

The Scriptures reveal how Jesus ministered healing to the sick, performing miracles and healing all who came to Him. God is and has always been the Healer. Repeated reference is made throughout the Word of God where Jesus healed *"all who came to Him,"* never refusing anyone or turning them away:

> *And Jesus went about all Galilee, teaching in their synagogues, preaching the gospel of the kingdom, and healing all kinds of sickness and all kinds of disease among the people. Then His fame went throughout all Syria; and they brought to Him all sick people who were afflicted with various diseases and torments, and those who were demon-possessed, epileptics,*

and paralytics; and He healed them. (Matthew 4:23-24) *When evening had come, they brought to Him many who were demon-possessed. And He cast out the spirits with a word, and healed all who were sick.* (Matthew 8:16)

But when Jesus knew it, he withdrew himself from thence: and great multitudes followed him, and he healed them all. (Matthew 12:15, KJV)

When the sun was setting, all those who had any that were sick with various diseases brought them to Him; and He laid His hands on every one of them and healed them. (Luke 4:40)

And He came down with them and stood on a level place with a crowd of His disciples and a great multitude of people from all Judea and Jerusalem, and from the seacoast of Tyre and Sidon, who came to hear Him and be healed of their diseases, as well as those who were tormented with unclean spirits. And they were healed. And the whole multitude sought to touch Him, for power went out from Him and healed them all. (Luke 6:17-19)

Now a woman, having a flow of blood for twelve years, who had spent all her livelihood on physicians and could not be healed by any.... Now when the woman saw that she was not hidden, she came trembling; and falling down before

Him, she declared to Him in the presence of all the people the reason she had touched Him and how she was healed immediately. (Luke 8:43, 47)

The Scriptures declare that Jesus went and healed all—not one, not two, not three, not ten, but all!

In addition to performing miracles of healing, Jesus also gave power to His disciples to heal, for the Bible declares: *"Then He called His twelve disciples together and gave them power and authority over all demons, and to cure diseases. He sent them to preach the kingdom of God and to heal the sick"* (Luke 9:1-2).

The Lord Jesus acknowledged that miracles help build faith: *"Then Jesus said to him, 'Unless you people see signs and wonders, you will by no means believe'"* (John 4:48). God promised to send forth believers: *"God also bearing witness both with signs and wonders, with various miracles, and gifts of the Holy Spirit, according to His own will"* (Hebrews 2:4).

Although the ministry of healing was demonstrated in different ways, the result was and is always the same: God does heal!

MIRACLES TODAY . . . AND YOU!

Today many believers acknowledge God's ability to do the miraculous. However, like the leper who came to Jesus in Matthew 8:1-5 begging for his healing, they pray, "If it be your will, Lord, heal me," they are not sure that it is God's will for them to be healed and to work miracles anymore.

God's will is not a mystery; it is clearly revealed in the Word of God. The leper did not know the will of God regarding the cleansing of his leprosy. That is why he fell at the feet of the Jesus Christ and worshiped, saying, *"And behold, a leper came and worshiped Him, saying, 'Lord, if You are willing, You can make me clean'"* (Matthew 8:2). Immediately Jesus stretched forth His hand and touched him, saying, *"Then Jesus put out His hand and touched him, saying, 'I am willing; be cleansed.' Immediately his leprosy was cleansed"* (Matthew 8:3).

Jesus was willing then, and He is willing today, for He declares: *"And whatever you ask in My name, that I will do, that the Father may be glorified in the Son. If you ask anything in My name, I will do it"* (John 14:13-14).

God's promises are timeless. When you bring your need for a miracle to the Lord, get rid of the "if" and pray in faith, expecting to receive! James 5:15 declares, *"And the prayer of faith will save the sick, and the Lord will raise him up."*

It is God's will for you to walk in the miraculous and a right relationship with Him: *"Beloved, I pray that you may prosper in all things and be in health, just as your soul prospers"* (3 John 2). God has not changed. According to Malachi 3:6, *"For I am the LORD, I do not change."*

Just as it was during the time when the Lord Jesus walked on this earth and those who saw Him witnessed signs, wonders, and miraculous acts, so it is today. Miracles still happen. Blind eyes still receive their sight. Deaf ears still begin to hear. The crippled and the lame still leap to their feet and walk.

The unchangeableness of God's character is certain. Whether a miracle happens instantaneously or by process of time, He is a God of signs and miracles—yesterday, today, and forever!

Best of all, you can be used to bring the marvelous and miraculous to others, for *"Most assuredly, I say to you, he who believes in Me, the works that I do he will do also; and greater works than these he will do, because I go to My Father"* (John 14:12).

8

GOD'S DIVINE PRESENCE

Then you shall know that I am in the midst of Israel:
I am the LORD your God
And there is no other.
My people shall never be put to shame.

—JOEL 2:27

This wonderful blessing of the Atonement means that everywhere you go, His presence goes with you. His presence is there to lead, to protect, to provide, to admonish, to teach—to do whatever is needed in your life at that moment.

When He says, "*My people shall never be put to shame,*" this means when God does His wondrous things in your life, you will be able to testify that it was God, not your own power, and that Isaiah's prophecy concerning the power, protection, and presence of God upon His people is at work in your life: "*No weapon formed against you shall prosper, and every tongue which rises against you in judgment you shall condemn. This is the heritage of the servants of the* LORD, *And their righteousness is from Me, says the* LORD*"* (Isaiah 54:17).

His presence is promised to you. He wants to encircle you everywhere you go. He longs to be there, wherever you are, so no enemy can hurt you.

GOD'S SANCTUARY

Go with me to a place where few enter, where you are saturated with the presence of God, where the glory is, where you are literally baptized in God's awesome power. You no longer feel guilty or confess sin. That was taken care of in the Outer Court. You pass through the Holy Place, where your soul begins to surrender to the will of the Father.

Then something miraculous happens. You go beyond the veil, into the Holy of Holies, deeper than ever with the Father. The flesh cannot enter; the soul can no longer talk or participate. Communion begins with your spirit. God begins speaking. His presence is so abundant that you can only listen. You must be quiet. In the presence of God, words are inadequate. You have entered into a higher revelation.

Quietness is all around you, but not as a sign of lack. It is a sign of abundance. Christ Jesus is no longer the Person about whom you've read. He becomes real, altogether lovely, the express image of God's glory. This is where He reveals Himself.

The wealth of His presence is beyond the veil. Your spirit becomes more alive than you ever dreamed possible, for it responds to the Creator. The depths and heights are unsearchable.

Your life is changed forever, yet it just beginning to change. You've begun to understand, in a small way, what David the psalmist was acknowledging when he wrote: *"You shall hide them in the secret place of Your presence from the plots of man; You shall keep them secretly in a pavilion from the strife of tongues"* (Psalm 31:20). It means total immersion. It means absolute protection. Sickness is not allowed there. Enemies of God cannot enter.

You lose track of time. God imparts things to you that are unspeakable. And when it is time to leave, you cannot wait to return, for you have just begun to dwell in presence of God. You have experienced a taste of what it will be when you are in heaven's throne room forever.

Few humans enter this sanctuary of God's presence. Why? The price is simply more than most people are willing to pay.

What Keeps You from God's Presence?

If God has promised His presence, why don't believers immerse themselves in Him more than they do? The answer is fairly predictable. We must spend time with Him! It is that simple.

A. W. Tozer, a powerful twentieth century prophet who has had a great impact on the body of Christ, once wrote:

> If we would progress spiritually, we must separate ourselves unto the things of God and concentrate upon them to the exclusion of a thousand things the worldly man considers important. We must cultivate God in the

solitudes and silence; we must make the kingdom of God
the sphere of our activity and labor in it like a farmer in
his field, like a miner in the earth. [1]

There is no other way to behold God's glory than to seek Him. In
John 17:24, Jesus prayed, *"Father, I desire that they also whom You gave
Me may be with Me where I am, that they may behold My glory which You
have given Me; for You loved Me before the foundation of the world."* Jesus
prayed that you would behold His glory! He longs for you to be with
Him. There should be nothing to separate you from Him.

You no longer have to depend upon the high priest to go into
the Holy of Holies, once a year during the Day of Atonement, on
your behalf any longer. The veil has been rent, and the way is open
for you to boldly approach the throne of grace.

He openly beckons you to come and be with Him: *"Abide in Me,
and I in you. As the branch cannot bear fruit of itself, unless it abides in
the vine, neither can you, unless you abide in Me"* (John 15:4). James 4:8
tells us, *"Draw near to God and He will draw near to you."*

A greater anointing will come upon you as you continue to abide
in the Lord. The same great power and anointing that came upon
David can pour out upon your life.

Smith Wigglesworth, a great evangelist of the early 1900s and a
man who knew the power of God's anointing said:

It is not sufficient just to have a touch of God or to
usually have a desire for God. There is only one thing
that will meet the needs of the people today, and that is
to be immersed in the life of God—God taking you and

filling you with His Spirit, until you live right in God, and God lives in you, so that *"whether you eat or drink, or whatever you do,"* it will all be for the *"glory of God"* (1 Corinthians 10:31). [2]

As Smith Wigglesworth described, are you hungry to be filled with God's Spirit? Are you ready to recover all as you move into an entirely new dimension of God's power? God wants you to be immersed in His presence today.

HUNGER AND THIRST

I often ask people, "What is the great desire of your heart?" Many say, "I want the presence of God in my life. I want to truly know Him."

If closeness with God is your desire, here's some wonderful news: He desires a close relationship with you, even more than you do.

From the beginning, the Father created Adam and Eve for fellowship. From the moment sin broke that fellowship, He offered ways to rebuild a loving relationship. Enoch is mentioned in the Bible simply for walking with God.

Down through the generations—through Abraham, Isaac, and Jacob—the Father continually and patiently drew people toward Him.

Think back for a moment to the time when Moses was given instructions for building the ark of the covenant:

You shall put the mercy seat on top of the ark, and in the ark you shall put the Testimony that I will give you. And there I

will meet with you, and I will speak with you from above the
mercy seat, from between the two cherubim which are on the
ark of the Testimony, about everything which I will give you in
commandment to the children of Israel. (Exodus 25:21-22).

God wanted to meet with Moses! Our heavenly Father wanted to talk with him. What a powerful portrayal of God's desire for fellowship.

Fast-forward to the time when Jesus was hanging on the cross of Calvary. The veil was split in two, from the top to the bottom, signaling His desire to allow all believers the authority to meet with Him. The Holy Spirit, likewise, was given so we could move into a new dimension of closeness and power. Today, God is available!

However, I know of only one way to know Him intimately: we must spend time with Him. There is no substitute. There are no shortcuts to intimacy with Him. We must hunger and thirst after Him.

But do you know what it means to hunger and thirst after God's presence? David, as he wrote the Psalms under the inspiration of the Holy Spirit, revealed such a longing for God's divine presence that it began to affect him physically. He felt the awesome presence of the Almighty in the temple, and he desired that same spirit to be an ongoing part of his private walk with God. Observe how David described the cry of his heart: *"As the deer pants for the water brooks, so pants my soul for You, O God."* (Psalm 42:1).

How deeply David desired to be close and intimate with the Lord. He used the word *pants* in describing his longing for God. That is the audible sound a deer makes when it is thirsty and searching for water. He said, *"My soul thirsts for God, for the living God"* (Psalm 42:2).

How often do you thirst for His presence? Obviously, David's soul was parched and craving. He knew that only by coming into the presence of the Lord would his longing be quenched.

Continuing in the same passage of Psalm 42, David wrote, *"Deep calls unto deep."* Can you hear the heartfelt cry of David pleading for a deeper fellowship with God? He longed to feel God's presence washing over him.

In Psalm 63, David continues his plea:

O God, You are my God;
Early will I seek You;
My soul thirsts for You;
My flesh longs for You
In a dry and thirsty land
Where there is no water.
So I have looked for You in the sanctuary,
To see Your power and Your glory.

Because Your lovingkindness is better than life,
My lips shall praise You.
Thus I will bless You while I live;
I will lift up my hands in Your name.
My soul shall be satisfied as with marrow and fatness,
And my mouth shall praise You with joyful lips.

When I remember You on my bed,
I meditate on You in the night watches.

Because You have been my help,
Therefore in the shadow of Your wings I will rejoice.
My soul follows close behind You;
Your right hand upholds me. (Psalm 63:1-8)

David knew how to seek, enter, and stay in God's holy presence. What a lesson for every believer! If we come to the place where we are as desperate and thirsty for God as David was, God will draw near to us.

You see, communication with the Father is not about merely saying prayers. Many sincere individuals spend a great amount of time creating a highly organized, lengthy prayer list. And their entire effort is spent going through the agenda—one petition after another. God wants us to spend time with Him, not listen to our "gimme" lists.

Your relationship with God is not a business strategy. You do not come into His presence through a ritual, but through a bond and growing relationship. Instead, fellowship with your heavenly Father is the natural result of a deep desire. It comes because you begin to pray, "Intensify my hunger, Lord. Increase my desire for You!"

It is your hunger that will help you move into God's presence. It is your thirst that will cause the waters from above to flood your soul afresh.

Fellowship is impossible without relationship. He touches you and you respond. Then as you reach out, He extends Himself to you. It all starts with a hunger and thirst for Him.

HEART TO HEART

Staying in God's presence is the outgrowth of a heart that is broken before the Lord. Your soul must cry out for God. Just as repentance is necessary for salvation, dependence is required for His continual presence.

When you totally yield yourself in the presence of the Lord, you move past praying and into a fellowship that cannot be described. You are communing with the Lord—heart to heart.

You must seek to become like the prophet Isaiah who wrote:

> *Yes, in the way of Your judgments,*
> *O LORD, we have waited for You;*
> *The desire of our soul is for Your name*
> *And for the remembrance of You.*
> *With my soul I have desired You in the night,*
> *Yes, by my spirit within me I will seek You early;*
> *For when Your judgments are in the earth,*
> *The inhabitants of the world will learn righteousness.* (Isaiah 26:8-9)

When you have said all you can say in the natural, the spirit within begins crying out to God. What a glorious power and presence is available to us! God waits every day to feel your hunger and longing for Him. Then He allows His power to flow through you!

SILENCE IN HIS PRESENCE

Somehow we have been taught that spending time in God's presence means talking on and on. We have placed such an importance on our own words and eloquent prayers. Nothing could be further from the truth. It is often our silence that the Lord desires. The prophet Zephaniah wrote, *"Be silent in the presence of the Lord GOD"* (Zephaniah 1:7).

Yes, there are times for you to speak, but as you spend time with Him, His abundance often leaves no room for words. Yet in your silence you are in total communication with the Lord. God's presence calms the soul and stills the activities of the flesh.

Too often we try to reach God through personal efforts and heartfelt prayers, but when you truly seek His presence, you know it is time to be silent. That is when true fellowship begins.

When God has your complete attention—when your mind is inactive and the flesh is not in control—the Lord will begin His fellowship with you. When quietness comes, the Spirit begins talking. If you truly want to spend time in His presence, He tells you to *"be still, and know that I am God"* (Psalm 46:10).

GOD'S TIMETABLE

When coming into God's presence, it is better to have a heart without words than words with no heart.

When I get alone with God and am ready to pray, I often say, "Father, Your Word says You will quicken us, then we can call upon You. Lord, I am waiting for Your quickening." Then I remain quiet until I sense the presence of God's Spirit.

"How long do you wait?" I've been asked.

"As long as it takes!"

You see, God doesn't exist to fit into our manmade schedules. The Lord is clear about whose timetable matters: *"And you will seek Me and find Me, when you search for Me with all your heart"* (Jeremiah 29:13).

Andrew Murray, a truly great man of prayer, once said that

before he sought to enter God's presence, he often said, "Lord, melt my cold heart. Break my hard heart and prepare it for Your touch."

Oh, that we would be willing to approach the Father in that way! The Bible declares that when the Holy Spirit comes in we cry, *"Abba, Father"* (Romans 8:15). This implies surrender to His will and His way of living. It means giving control to Him. As the Spirit of God comes in, He begins to remove our weakness. He roots out the barriers to a loving, close relationship with the Father.

How Will Your Life Change?

Being in God's holy presence will transform you in more wonderful ways than you can imagine:

God's anointing will be poured out upon you to keep you and protect from the world. Earthly things will matter less and less.

Jesus will be exalted in your life. An abundance of praise and worship will stream through your life when you are filled with His presence, and our precious Lord Jesus is exalted when God's people are filled. You will overflow in praise. As God touches your life more and more, everything in you will reach out to Him.

Your prayer life will be intensified. God's presence gives you a better understanding of what it means to pray in union with His desires. You can pray from your innermost being rather than from your mind. It moves you from mere human communication into a supernatural realm:

> *Likewise the Spirit also helps in our weaknesses. For we do not know what we should pray for as we ought, but the*

Spirit Himself makes intercession for us with groanings which cannot be uttered. Now He who searches the hearts knows what the mind of the Spirit is, because He makes intercession for the saints according to the will of God. (Romans 8:26-27)

Your desire to know Him more through the Bible will be deepened and strengthened. At the same time, the Word will cause you to want to spend more time in His presence. The Holy Spirit will literally make the Word of God come alive in you: *"But the Helper, the Holy Spirit, whom the Father will send in My name, He will teach you all things, and bring to your remembrance all things that I said to you"* (John 14:26). The Spirit of God increases your knowledge of the Word and brings it to life so you can apply it to your daily walk in Christ Jesus.

He will help you, lead you, and guide your steps. He will help you make decisions, both great and small, which will increasingly affect your life: *"For as many as are led by the Spirit of God, these are sons of God"* (Romans 8:14). He will keep you from making wrong decisions. God will infuse you with His wisdom and insight: *"I will instruct you and teach you in the way you should go"* (Psalm 32:8).

You will experience divine life. You will be raised up as He dwells increasingly in you: *"But if the Spirit of Him who raised Jesus from the dead dwells in you, He who raised Christ from the dead will also give life to your mortal bodies through His Spirit who dwells in you"* (Romans 8:11).

Best of all, spending time in God's presence will help you understand more of the coming glory. Spending time in God's presence is not literally the same as entering into the actual throne room in heaven, but it does give you a taste of your coming inheritance in Christ Jesus. It is like a down payment. God gives us a glorious taste of what is coming in eternity, and that foretaste causes you to seek more and more of His presence!

His presence will lead you to higher ground right now. His presence will bring clarity to your mind and a new fire to your heart. All you must do to receive it is yield to the Lord and spend time with Him.

INTIMACY

What would your life be like if you could move into the powerful, overwhelming, all-encompassing, eternal presence of God without fail, anytime you desired? How different would your life be? your conversations? your relationships? your thoughts? your goals? your actions?

It is possible to enjoy the presence of God every day, to be ushered into the Holy of Holies.

No matter what's going on in your life right now, be encouraged. There is hope. The questions at this point are simple: Are you willing to hunger and thirst for the presence of God? Are you willing to make your relationship with Him the most important part of your life? Are you willing to pay the price for such a wonderful union with Him?

Only then can you begin to know God in His fullness. Only then will you truly move into the fifth blessing of the Atonement—God's divine presence.

9

BLESSINGS UPON YOUR FAMILY

And it shall come to pass afterward
That I will pour out My Spirit on all flesh;
Your sons and your daughters shall prophesy,
Your old men shall dream dreams,
Your young men shall see visions.
And also on My menservants and on My maidservants
I will pour out My Spirit in those days.
And I will show wonders in the heavens and in the earth.

—JOEL 2:28-30

Do you realize that God loves your family even more than you do? That comes as a surprise to some people, especially those who are struggling with unbelieving sons, daughters, and grandchildren. Our heavenly Father is concerned for your family in so many ways:

- It is God's desire for your family to build a great heritage: "*May the LORD give you increase more and more, you and your children*" (Psalm 115:14).

- It is God's desire to prosper you and your loved ones: *"Praise the LORD! Blessed is the man who fears the LORD, who delights greatly in His commandments. His descendants will be mighty on earth; the generation of the upright will be blessed. Wealth and riches will be in his house, and his righteousness endures forever"* (Psalm 112:1-3).

- It is God's will for all to be saved and to serve Him. The Word declares: *"The Lord is…not willing that any should perish, but that all should come to repentance"* (2 Peter 3:9).

- And it is God's will for you and your children to receive Him as your personal Savior and follow Him all your days: *"Believe on the Lord Jesus Christ, and you will be saved, you and your household"* (Acts 16:31).

The sixth blessing of the Atonement applies directly to you and your loved ones. Is it any wonder why Satan and his evil forces have historically hated this institution? Is it any wonder why recent years have seen a global explosion of attacks on the family?

Enough!

It is time for the demonic powers that have encroached on our families to move over. God has given so many promises concerning our households. If your loved ones are not where they need to be spiritually, you can be encouraged. Your groanings have not gone unheard. Your agonizing prayers will be answered. The power of God is coming in like a flood to rescue your loved ones.

Salvation and blessing should start at home. It begins with

your sons, daughters, your husband, wife, mother, and father. Then we must reach out to our extended family members—uncles, aunts, cousins and grandparents—our neighbors and to all those we love.

There are numerous examples throughout the Old and New Testaments.

SAFE IN THE ARK

Why do you think God asked Noah to build the ark? If you think it was to save all the animals, you are right, but only partially right.

God actually had the ark prepared for Noah and his family. Skeptical? Read Hebrews 11:7: *"By faith Noah, being divinely warned of things not yet seen, moved with godly fear, prepared an ark for the saving of his household, by which he condemned the world and became heir of the righteousness which is according to faith."*

What faith Noah had! People living in his day had not seen water fall from the sky and this man declared, "It is going to rain, and the whole world will be flooded!"

Quickly, he began building an ark to save his family from something he could hardly describe. "Oh, you foolish man," the people must have laughed.

In a world filled with iniquity, there was only one person who found grace in the eyes of the Lord—Noah (Genesis 6:8). The Lord said to Noah, *"Come into the ark, you and all your household, because I have seen that you are righteous before Me in this generation"* (Genesis 7:1). It was Noah's faith that allowed his family to be saved. Centuries later, Peter wrote that God *"did not spare the ancient world, but saved*

Noah, one of eight people, a preacher of righteousness, bringing in the flood on the world of the ungodly" (2 Peter 2:5).

Is the Lord concerned about your family? You can count on it! Each member of your household has a free will whether to accept the Father's call, just as Noah's sons—Shem, Ham, and Japheth—could have chosen to opt out of their family's salvation plan. Still, when you are righteous before the Lord, your entire family will be touched and beckoned by God's amazing grace.

It is God's desire to protect and bless the entire household.

A LAMB FOR A HOUSE

In the Old Testament, as part of the original instructions for the feasts, God commanded Moses to speak to the people of Israel about God's concern for the salvation of the whole family:

> *Speak to all the congregation of Israel, saying: "On the tenth day of this month every man shall take for himself a lamb, according to the house of his father, a lamb for a household. And if the household is too small for the lamb, let him and his neighbor next to his house take it according to the number of the persons; according to each man's need you shall make your count for the lamb."* (Exodus 12:3-4)

During the Passover feast, it is the tradition that every Jewish family takes one lamb for a family, and if one partakes, all are to partake. The lamb is available for the entire house. God's intention, from the first Passover, was for a lamb to be sacrificed for each house. It wasn't a lamb for each person. The shed blood was to cover every person in the household. It wasn't just the father, but fathers. It wasn't just the mother, but mothers. The protection included uncles, aunts, and cousins. And notice in verse 4, the neighbors could even be protected by the shed blood of the lamb.

Are you beginning to grasp how your family has special privileges because you have been saved? The Bible is filled with numerous examples of household salvation.

Certainly, every person in the household had the free choice of whether to stay in the house which was protected by the blood, just as each individual in a house has free will to decide whether to accept Jesus Christ as Savior, and just as each person has the choice of whether to receive each of the seven blessings of the Atonement.

THE PRISON GUARD

On the authority of God's Word, you not only can claim salvation for your household, but you can also see them born again. One of the great revelations of God's Word is that salvation is promised not only for an individual but for the entire household. Look for a moment at the story of Paul and Silas, who were beaten and thrown into prison for preaching the Gospel. The jailer was instructed to keep them secure, so he placed them in an inner prison and bound their feet with chains.

How did Paul and Silas respond? At midnight they *were praying and singing hymns to God, and the prisoners were listening to them"* (Acts 16:25).

Suddenly there was a great earthquake. The foundations of the prison were shaken, and immediately all the doors were opened and everyone's chains were loosed:

"And the keeper of the prison, awaking from sleep and seeing the prison doors open, supposing the prisoners had fled, drew his sword and was about to kill himself" (Acts 16:27).

Why was the jailer about to take such drastic action? Under Roman law if you guarded a prisoner who escaped, you were required to give your life for that fugitive. It would be easier to take his own life rather than to face the courts and be killed. If he did not, one of his family members would be substituted for the execution.

Imagine his surprise at what happened next. The Bible tells us that Paul called with a loud voice, saying, *"Do yourself no harm, for we are all here"* (Acts 16:28). In the darkness, the jailer called for a light, ran in, and fell down trembling before Paul and Silas. He brought them out, saying, *"Sirs, what must I do to be saved?"* (verse 30).

Why would he ask such a remarkable question? That guard heard the two Christians singing and praising God in the night and was drawn by the Holy Spirit to seek the Savior. Then Paul and Silas gave the jailer this marvelous assurance: *"Believe on the Lord Jesus Christ, and you will be saved, you and your household"* (Acts 16:31).

Think of it! Salvation was not only for this man, but it was meant for his entire household. And look at what happened: *"Then they spoke the word of the Lord to him and to all who were in his house"* (Acts 16:32).

What a mighty God we serve! He is concerned about your whole family!

GOD LOVES FAMILIES

Acts 16 shares another story where the household is mentioned prominently:

> *Now a certain woman named Lydia heard us. She was a seller of purple from the city of Thyatira, who worshiped God. The Lord opened her heart to heed the things spoken by Paul. And when she and her household were baptized, she begged us, saying, "If you have judged me to be faithful to the Lord, come to my house and stay." So she persuaded us.* (Acts 16:14-15)

Lydia was originally from Thyatira (where one of the seven churches of Asia were later located) but was a resident in Philippi, in Greece, when the apostle Paul traveled there on his first missionary journey. Although she is mentioned only briefly in the Scriptures, she holds a prominent place in Bible history, since she is the first recorded Christian in Europe. Her family was saved, as well, and her home became the place where the first church in Europe gathered to worship.

Another interesting story concerns the ruler of the synagogue: *"Then Crispus, the ruler of the synagogue, believed on the Lord with all his household. And many of the Corinthians, hearing, believed and were baptized"* (Acts 18:8).

God loves the family!

HOUSEHOLD BLESSINGS

You have the legal right, based upon God's Word, to claim every member of your family for Christ. You have the same right to claim salvation for your neighbors. You also have the honor of claiming the seven blessings of the Atonement.

Charles H. Spurgeon, one of history's greatest Bible teachers, preached often about God's blessing on the family, including these powerful words:

> It sometimes happens that a good man has to go alone to heaven: God's election has separated him from the midst of an ungodly family, and, notwithstanding his example and his prayers, and his admonitions, they still remain unconverted, and he himself, a solitary one, a speckled bird amongst them, has to pursue his lonely flight to the skies. Far oftener, however, it happens that the God who is the God of Abraham becomes the God of Sarah, and then of Isaac, and then of Jacob, and though grace does not run in the blood, and regeneration is not of blood nor of birth, yet doth it very frequently—I was about to say almost always—happen that God, by means of one of a household, draws the rest to himself. He calls an individual, and then uses him to be a sort of spiritual decoy to bring the rest of the family into the gospel net. [1]

The promises are yours. There is an umbrella of grace over you and your household. You can build a powerful heritage, starting with your loved ones.

Just remember that the secret for all the Atonement season blessings is this: *"They shall not appear before the LORD empty-handed"* (Deuteronomy 16:16).

Come with your Atonement offering. Prove God. Claim each of your loved ones for the Lord. Then watch Him pour out more blessings than you can hold. See Him bless your family.

Amazing things are just ahead! Are you ready?

10

DELIVERANCE

And it shall come to pass
That whoever calls on the name of the LORD
Shall be saved.
For in Mount Zion and in Jerusalem there shall be
  deliverance,
As the LORD has said,
Among the remnant whom the LORD calls.

—JOEL 2:32

Joel 2:32 holds the seventh promise God made to those who honor the Atonement Day. You can call upon the name of the Lord Jesus for deliverance—wherever you are, whatever time it is, and no matter the overwhelming challenges you face.

Yes Joel 2 specifically mentions Mount Zion and Jerusalem, but for those of us who have been "grafted" as wild olive branches into the tree (Romans 11:11-24), the promise of deliverance is available to believers everywhere!

You can seek deliverance from Satan's attacks whether you are driving on the Autobahn or the back streets of your city or town. As Gordon Jensen once penned in his classic song, "He's as close as the mention of His name." God promised to be there when you need Him in the middle of the night when your child has a raging fever. Just call. He will be there. He will bring deliverance.

When you are either figuratively or literally fighting for your life, He will be there. He promised. He will deliver you. When you are in your own personal lion's den or fiery furnace, His deliverance—as promised—will be there for you.

JOSEPH'S DELIVERANCE

You may ask, "When will it happen? When will I receive deliverance?"

Let me share with you one of my favorite lessons in Scripture, the story of Joseph, the seventeen-year-old son of Jacob who had a marvelous dream from God.

In his dream he saw himself as a great ruler, with even his own brothers bowing down to him. It was almost more than they could handle. You see, his eleven brothers were extremely jealous of Joseph. He had been born when Jacob was quite old and the father gave only him a richly ornamented robe, a coat of many colors. It was a garment to be worn by a king.

The Bible tells us that *"when his brothers saw that their father loved him more than all his brothers, they hated him and could not speak peaceably to him"* (Genesis 37:4).

Then Joseph seemingly made things worse for himself when he told his brothers about his dream:

> *"Please hear this dream which I have dreamed: There we were, binding sheaves in the field. Then behold, my sheaf arose and also stood upright; and indeed your sheaves stood all around and bowed down to my sheaf." And his brothers said to him, "Shall you indeed reign over us? Or shall you indeed have dominion over us?" So they hated him even more for his dreams and for his words.* (Genesis 37:6-8)

You undoubtedly know how the rest of the story goes. One day, when Joseph's brothers were in the field grazing the flocks of the father, they devised a plan to kill him: *"Now when they saw him afar off, even before he came near them, they conspired against him to kill him. Then they said to one another, 'Look, this dreamer is coming! Come therefore, let us now kill him and cast him into some pit; and we shall say, 'Some wild beast has devoured him.' We shall see what will become of his dreams!"* (Genesis 37:18-20).

The brothers stripped him of the colorful robe and threw him into a cistern, fully intending that he would die in that empty pit.

Then, as they sat down to eat their meal they saw a caravan of Ishmaelites passing by on their way to Egypt to sell their goods and spices. One of the brothers had an idea: *"So Judah said to his brothers, 'What profit is there if we kill our brother and conceal his blood? Come and let us sell him to the Ishmaelites, and let not our hand be upon him, for he is our brother and our flesh.' And his brothers listened"*

(Genesis 37:26-27). His brothers agreed and sold Joseph into slavery for twenty shekels of silver.

The brothers deceived their father, Jacob, concerning the incident. In their shame, the brothers slaughtered a goat and rubbed blood on Joseph's robe. And when they brought the special garment to Jacob, he recognized it immediately and was filled with unbearable sorrow:

> So they took Joseph's tunic, killed a kid of the goats, and dipped the tunic in the blood. Then they sent the tunic of many colors, and they brought it to their father and said, "We have found this. Do you know whether it is your son's tunic or not?"
>
> And he recognized it and said, "It is my son's tunic. A wild beast has devoured him. Without doubt Joseph is torn to pieces." Then Jacob tore his clothes, put sackcloth on his waist, and mourned for his son many days. And all his sons and all his daughters arose to comfort him; but he refused to be comforted, and he said, "For I shall go down into the grave to my son in mourning." Thus his father wept for him. (Genesis 37:31-35)

Joseph needed deliverance many times during the ensuing years. He was a slave in Egypt, yet the vision God had placed within him would not die. Even when he was a prisoner in the house of Potiphar, he knew that somehow, some way, he would become a great ruler—just as the Lord had revealed. More prison time came, then the events that happened next changed Joseph's life dramatically. Because of his ability to interpret dreams, he was brought from his prison cell, directly into the court of Pharaoh. God not only allowed Joseph to correctly explain the king's dream, but Pharaoh subsequently named him to be governor of the nation! Deliverance had come to Joseph, but deliverance for others was just beginning.

A great famine began to ravage the land, spreading to Canaan. Jacob sent his sons on an expedition to Egypt to purchase the grain they so desperately needed. They had no idea that the only person who could approve the purchase was their own brother:

> *Joseph saw his brothers and recognized them, but he acted as a stranger to them and spoke roughly to them. Then he said to them, "Where do you come from?"*
>
> *And they said, "From the land of Canaan to buy food."*
> *So Joseph recognized his brothers, but they did not recognize him. Then Joseph remembered the dreams which he had dreamed about them.* (Genesis 42:7-9)

In the presence of this man they thought was a total stranger, the brothers began to fear for their lives. They were filled with remorse:

> *Then they said to one another, "We are truly guilty concerning our brother, for we saw the anguish of his soul when he pleaded with us, and we would not hear; therefore this distress has come upon us.*
>
> *"And Reuben answered them, saying, "Did I not speak*

to you, saying, 'Do not sin against the boy'; and you would
not listen? Therefore behold, his blood is now required of us."
But they did not know that Joseph understood them, for he
spoke to them through an interpreter. (Genesis 42:21-23)

Finally, on a subsequent visit, when Joseph revealed himself, they were terrified even more. Yet he comforted his brothers, saying, *"But now, do not therefore be grieved or angry with yourselves because you sold me here; for God sent me before you to preserve life"* (Genesis 45:5). Joseph knew that because he was governor of Egypt, he was in the position to save Canaan from this horrible famine.

He had been delivered and had become an instrument of deliverance for His family and entire nations!

With a spiritual maturity and insight seasoned by years and years of struggle, Joseph responded in a remarkable way when his brothers fell before him and offered to become his slaves. He told them: *"But as for you, you meant evil against me; but God meant it for good, in order to bring it about as it is this day, to save many people alive"* (Genesis 50:20).

Joseph was placed in the palace for deliverance!

Spiritual Warfare

The problem with deliverance is not God. We are the ones who have been negligent in recognizing the fact that we are engaged in a spiritual battle, a conflict of the ages. This truth has not been hidden from us because

Jesus wanted us in the dark, but it has been hidden from us because we are so slow of heart to believe! It has been difficult to accept because we have an enemy who does not want us to understand, trust in and walk in this truth! Jesus said, *"If you abide in My word, you are My disciples indeed. And you shall know the truth, and the truth shall make you free"* (John 8:31-32).

Here are several basic truths that He gave us concerning our battle with the kingdom of darkness:

- *"Behold, I give you the authority to trample on serpents and scorpions, and over all the power of the enemy, and nothing shall by any means hurt you"* (Luke 10:19).

- *"And I will give you the keys of the kingdom of heaven, and whatever you bind on earth will be bound in heaven, and whatever you loose on earth will be loosed in heaven"* (Matthew 16:19). On the cross Jesus announced, "It is finished!" referring to His finished work in redeeming mankind. He immediately descended into the habitat of the enemy returning with the keys of death and Hades. Satan no longer has rightful ownership of even that which he is prince over! The battle is won!

- We are clearly and emphatically told about our weapons of war in 2 Corinthians 10:3-4: *"For though we walk in the flesh, we do not war according to the flesh. For the weapons of our warfare are not carnal but mighty in God for pulling down strongholds."*

In Ephesians Paul points out that we are engaged in a spiritual battle with the kingdom of darkness, and we are given explicit directions on the identification, care, and purpose of our weapons of war:

> *Finally, my brethren, be strong in the Lord and in the power of His might. Put on the whole armor of God, that you may be able to stand against the wiles of the devil. For we do not wrestle against flesh and blood, but against principalities, against powers, against the rulers of the darkness of this age, against spiritual hosts of wickedness in the heavenly places. Therefore take up the whole armor of God, that you may be able to withstand in the evil day, and having done all, to stand.*
>
> *Stand therefore, having girded your waist with truth, having put on the breastplate of righteousness, and having shod your feet with the preparation of the gospel of peace; above all, taking the shield of faith with which you will be able to quench all the fiery darts of the wicked one. And take the helmet of salvation, and the sword of the Spirit, which is the word of God; praying always with all prayer and supplication in the Spirit, being watchful to this end with all perseverance and supplication for all the saints.* (Ephesians 6:10-18)

Armed with these truths we are faced with an incredible adventure of deliverance, we know that *"the weapons of our warfare are not carnal but mighty in God for pulling down strongholds"* (2 Corinthians 10:4).

God not only desires to deliver us, but, as with Joseph, He

wants us to be part of the deliverance army as we pull down those strongholds of the enemy.

A Deadly Enemy . . . a Powerful Deliverer

We need God's deliverance! This is reality: A deadly enemy lurks out there who would love for you to believe he doesn't exist.

Here is the greater reality: God and His forces are more powerful than Satan and his army to deliver us. We can take the authority of God's Word and cast the devil's forces out. Over and over, Jesus ministered deliverance: *"When evening had come, they brought to Him many who were demon-possessed. And He cast out the spirits with a word, and healed all who were sick"* (Matthew 8:16).

Then, before He ascended to heaven, Jesus said:

> *Go into all the world and preach the gospel to every creature. He who believes and is baptized will be saved; but he who does not believe will be condemned. And these signs will follow those who believe: In My name they will cast out demons; they will speak with new tongues; they will take up serpents; and if they drink anything deadly, it will by no means hurt them; they will lay hands on the sick, and they will recover.* (Mark 16:15-18)

You have been issued your marching orders. As a believer, you not only are delivered, but you are to be an instrument of deliverance.

God desires that His power might flow through you. We are in combat with the forces of darkness. The Lord has called you to be a soldier in the conflict of the ages:

> *You therefore, my son, be strong in the grace that is in Christ Jesus. And the things that you have heard from me among many witnesses, commit these to faithful men who will be able to teach others also. You therefore must endure hardship as a good soldier of Jesus Christ. No one engaged in warfare entangles himself with the affairs of this life, that he may please him who enlisted him as a soldier.* (2 Timothy 2:1-4)

Do you realize the power that is available to you?

> *Therefore I also, after I heard of your faith in the Lord Jesus and your love for all the saints, do not cease to give thanks for you, making mention of you in my prayers: that the God of our Lord Jesus Christ, the Father of glory, may give to you the spirit of wisdom and revelation in the knowledge of Him, the eyes of your understanding being enlightened; that you may know what is the hope of His calling, what are the riches of the glory of His inheritance in the saints, and what is the exceeding greatness of His power toward us who believe, according to the working of His mighty power.* (Ephesians 1:15-19)

As believers we are co-heirs of God's rule and authority in His deliverance army, not weaklings who are afraid of our own shadows.

We have been saved for a purpose and endued with His power for a purpose:

> But God, who is rich in mercy, because of His great love with which He loved us, even when we were dead in trespasses, made us alive together with Christ (by grace you have been saved), and raised us up together, and made us sit together in the heavenly places in Christ Jesus, that in the ages to come He might show the exceeding riches of His grace in His kindness toward us in Christ Jesus. (Ephesians 2:4-7)

The problem is that too many Christians have allowed Satan to keep them in a perpetual state of worry and anxiety. They fail to comprehend that God is ready to fight our battles and deliver us.

The Lord promises us: *"I will give peace in the land, and you shall lie down, and none will make you afraid; I will rid the land of evil beasts, and the sword will not go through your land. You will chase your enemies, and they shall fall by the sword before you"* (Leviticus 26:6-7).

Now it is up to you to take authority over Satan and his army of demons. Unsheathe your spiritual swords and slay them, using God's deliverance power. That's how you fulfill the promise that *"five of you shall chase a hundred, and a hundred of you shall put ten thousand to flight; your enemies shall fall by the sword before you"* (Leviticus 26:8).

FIGHTING ON YOUR KNEES

One of the great deliverance lessons in the Bible is that we must win the battles in the spiritual realm before we can be victorious in physical battles and deliverance. It was a divine lesson learned by Moses, Elijah, and Joshua.

Regardless of how the devil may be enraged against you or why you need deliverance, God is on your side. He says:

> *Fear not, for I am with you; be not dismayed, for I am your God. I will strengthen you, Yes, I will help you, I will uphold you with My righteous right hand. Behold, all those who were incensed against you shall be ashamed and disgraced; they shall be as nothing, and those who strive with you shall perish.* (Isaiah 41:10-11)

One of the best ways to seek deliverance and fight spiritual battles is through prayer. Prayer is warfare, and it is won by an army marching on its knees. After all, God didn't tell us we would fight a war standing on earthly ground with physical swords. No! *"For the weapons of our warfare are not carnal but mighty in God for pulling down strongholds"* (2 Corinthians 10:4).

Certainly there will be times when you say, "Well, I don't feel like spending time on my knees." The way you feel is not the determining factor. Deliverance, spiritual warfare, and prayer are born out of your choices and not your emotions. The Bible declares, *"The effective, fervent prayer of a righteous man avails much"* (James 5:16).

Satan has no weapons against a warrior who simply won't give up, so don't stop praying. This is war! This is a battle for deliverance!

More than ever, we need to hear, as King Solomon did right after dedicating the temple, these words of the Lord: *"If My people who are called by My name will humble themselves, and pray and seek My face, and turn from their wicked ways, then I will hear from heaven, and will forgive their sin and heal their land"* (2 Chronicles 7:14).

Proverbs 21:31 tells us, *"The horse is prepared for the day of battle, but deliverance is of the LORD."*

Philippians 1:19 declares, *"For I know that this will turn out for my deliverance through your prayer and the supply of the Spirit of Jesus Christ."*

Deliverance is needed now, more than ever. Deliverance warriors are needed more than ever before.

Deliverance is the seventh blessing of the Atonement. Just remember, the conflict of the ages, our greatest challenge, our battle for deliverance, must first be waged on our knees!

PART THREE

GREATER THINGS

11

YOUR NEW COVENANT
OF ATONEMENT

*So he shall make atonement for the Holy Place, because of
the uncleanness of the children of Israel, and because of their
transgressions, for all their sins; and so he shall do for the
tabernacle of meeting which remains among them in the
midst of their uncleanness.*

—LEVITICUS 16:16

Why did Jesus Christ willingly come to earth, live a perfect life,
begin a public ministry at thirty years of age, then lay down His life
as a ransom for our sins?

Why?

The subject is so eternally huge that volumes of books could
not fully answer that question. He loved us, certainly. But why that
much? He gave His life as our sacrifice, but why would He do that?

I honestly couldn't offer up any of my children as a living
sacrifice for someone I dearly loved. It's unthinkable. It's especially

unfathomable to think that Christ came to earth to love the unlovable that resides in each of us.

Dr. Billy Graham, one of history's greatest evangelists, offered this explanation in his classic book *Peace with God*:

He, and He alone, had the power and capacity to bring man back to God. But would He? If He did, He would have to come to earth. He would have to take the form of a servant. He would have to humble Himself and become obedient unto death. He would have to grapple with sin. He would have to meet and overcome Satan, the enemy of man's souls. He would have to redeem sinners out of the slave market of sin. He would have to loose the bonds and set the prisoners free by paying a price—that price would be His own life. He would have to be despised and rejected of men, a man of sorrows and acquainted with grief. He would have to be smitten of God and separated from God. He would have to be wounded for the transgressions of men and bruised for their iniquities, His blood shed to atone for man's sin. He would have to reconcile God and man. He would be the great Mediator of history. He would have to be a substitute. He would have to die in the place of sinful man. All this would have to be done—voluntarily. [1]

Under the Old Covenant, God told His people to offer sacrifices to atone for sins once a year. These slain animals symbolically bore the punishment for sin that the people actually deserved. These sacrifices had to be made again and again. You see, this Old Covenant was only a glimpse of what would come later:

> *For the law, having a shadow of the good things to come, and not the very image of the things, can never with these same sacrifices, which they offer continually year by year, make those who approach perfect. For then would they not have ceased to be offered? For the worshipers, once purified, would have had no more consciousness of sins. But in those sacrifices there is a reminder of sins every year.* (Hebrews 10:1-3)

Jesus brought the New Covenant when He died for our sins: *"Then He said, 'Behold, I have come to do Your will, O God.' He takes away the first that He may establish the second. By that will we have been sanctified through the offering of the body of Jesus Christ once for all"* (Hebrews 10:9-10).

When Jesus shed His blood on the cross of Calvary, He sacrificed Himself *"once for all."* He said, *"It is finished"* (John 19:30), not "to be continued." The Bible declares that Jesus is *"the First and the Last,"* (Revelation 1:17) and He is *"the author and finisher of our faith"* (Hebrews 12:2).

Even though we still can partake of the seven blessings of the Atonement, you and I are no longer under the law. We have been offered grace instead. He came to die to take away all sin from you and me. He erased all our sins, blotted out all guilt, offered ultimate victory over death.

The Lord endured the passion on Calvary's cross to provide each of us with an eternal promise: *"But now He has obtained a more excellent ministry, inasmuch as He is also Mediator of a better covenant, which was established on better promises"* (Hebrews 8:6). We still have the blessings of the Old Covenant, but we also have the provisions of the New Covenant, all because of what He did on the cross.

What Happened on the Cross?

What actually happened on the cross? If you have seen the movie, *The Passion of the Christ*, you probably still have those scenes imbedded in your thoughts.

I think it is good to be reminded of what Jesus actually did for us as He endured the shame of our sins while nailed to the crossed timbers on Golgotha's hill. Maxwell Whyte could bring you to tears with his description of what happened that day. Let me share a couple of paragraphs from his book *The Power of the Blood*:

> Imagine, if you can, the scene of Calvary. No artist has ever pictured the Calvary scene as it really was. It would be too repulsive to paint on any canvas. It is doubtful that the Romans left Jesus even the courtesy of a loincloth…the crown of thorns was then put upon His head, not gently but roughly; many thorns (maybe a dozen or more), one-and-a-half inches long, jabbed into His scalp, producing such serious wounds that trickles of blood spurted out and ran into His hair and beard, matting both in dark red. The spikes were driven into the palms of His hands, and His blood coursed down His arms and sides. (Later the spear was thrust into His side

and His blood spilled out and ran down the sides of the cross onto the ground beneath.) Spikes were also driven through his feet and more blood ran down the sides of the cross on behalf of the sins of the whole world.

His bones were out of joint. (See Psalm 22.) His face was dreadful to look upon. There was no beauty in Him that we should desire Him (Isaiah 53:2). God gave His best, His Son, His perfect sacrifice—and even in death, there was no blemish in Him, for He was already dead when the soldiers arrived to break His legs, therefore, not a bone of Him was broken. Those who looked on Him saw only blood. It was a spectacle of blood. His hair and beard were soaked in His own blood. His back was lacerated from the thirty-nine stripes and was covered with His own blood. Even the cross was covered with blood, and the very earth was soaked. Every type of the atonement was fulfilled in Christ. [2]

Historians, archeologists, scientists, and forensic experts have examined in graphic detail the crucifixion of Jesus Christ. Virtually all have described His voluntary death as undoubtedly one of the most punishing and excruciating ways to carry out capital punishment ever devised by man.

Even before He went to the cross, Jesus was under tremendous, inhuman pressure: *"And being in agony, He prayed more earnestly. Then His sweat became like great drops of blood falling down to the ground"* (Luke 22:44). Today's medical experts have a term, *hematohidrosis*, which happens after severe inner stress causes the microscopic blood vessels to mix with sweat. It is related to being totally exhausted. People who experience this condition must receive fluids immediately or risk going into shock. Jesus, to our knowledge, did not drink anything before His arrest and torture.

After that arrest, Christ was beaten by the Jews, then scourged by the Roman soldiers. Historians, apart from biblical accounts, have documented these torturous beatings. Roman soldiers were especially brutal, deliberately lashed their whips to lacerate each victim's flesh in the most extremely painful manner.

Fluids often began building up around the heart and lungs after such horrific beatings. Lesser men died from this torture. Yet the torment was just beginning for Christ. The crown of thorns could have easily caused nerve damage in His head during the hours that passed. The brutal torture undoubtedly led to shock. How the Savior endured the loss of bodily fluid with no food or nourishment is beyond description.

Then He was forced to carry His own cross up Calvary's hill. How was He able to do this? Love for you and me, alone, kept Him going.

Nailed to those rough timbers as the cross slammed into the earth, Jesus somehow endured the hours that followed despite undoubtedly having to pull Himself upward to take each precious, ragged breath. Roman crosses were designed that way to produce the ultimate suffering for all to see so no thinking person who witnessed such a death would consider any crime against the state. Every movement certainly sent dizzying jolts of throbbing pain throughout His body. How Christ kept breathing, much less remain conscious, is beyond medical explanation. Normally the heart would fail from all the stress, but still He lived, hanging in shame, hour after hour.

It was no coincidence that at the exact hour of the day appointed in the Jewish temple for a sacrificial lamb to be killed, the end came for the Son of Man:

> *Now when the sixth hour had come, there was darkness over the whole land until the ninth hour. And at the ninth hour Jesus cried out with a loud voice, saying, "Eloi, Eloi, lama sabachthani?" which is translated, "My God, My God, why have You forsaken Me?" Some of those who stood by, when they heard that, said, "Look, He is calling for Elija" Then someone ran and filled a sponge full of sour wine, put it on a reed, and offered it to Him to drink, saying, "Let Him alone; let us see if Elijah will come to take Him down." And Jesus cried out with a loud voice, and breathed His last. Then the veil of the temple was torn in two from top to bottom. (Mark 15:33-38)*

As the temple's priestly ram's horn blew, signifying the completion of the priest's sacrifice of the lamb for the sins of Israel, Jesus breathed His last breath as a human. And at that same instant, it is recorded that the thick curtain that separated the Holy of Holies from the remainder of the temple, ripped from top to bottom.

> *Then the soldiers came and broke the legs of the first and of the other who was crucified with Him. But when they came*

to Jesus and saw that He was already dead, they did not break His legs. But one of the soldiers pierced His side with a spear, and immediately blood and water came out. And he who has seen has testified, and his testimony is true; and he knows that he is telling the truth, so that you may believe. For these things were done that the Scripture should be fulfilled, "Not one of His bones shall be broken." And again another Scripture says, "They shall look on Him whom they pierced." (John 19:32-37)

When the Roman soldier pierced Christ's left side, the wound allowed mingled blood and water to flow forth. Medical authorities say this is fairly common with cardiac rupture, or broken, burst heart. The beatings took an awful toll. The hours on the cross filled Him with immeasurable pain. Yet it was His choice, as He took all the sins of the world upon Him, that He willingly died as His heart apparently exploded.

How deep His grief! How unthinkable the pain! How great a love!

THE MESSAGE OF THE CROSS

When we gaze through the centuries at what happened on Calvary's cross, we see three things:

- The horrible, death-causing sin of mankind was nailed with Jesus on the cross. The Roman soldiers and the people of that day were not the only ones responsible for the crucifixion of our Savior. All of mankind, including you and me, are equally as guilty, for it was our sins—yours and mine—collectively and individually, that caused Jesus to come to earth and give Himself willingly as the ultimate sacrifice.

- God's love is overwhelming. It is on the cross where both God the Father and Jesus His Son gave history's greatest gift.

- The Savior willingly gave Himself as the only means to the Father: *"Jesus saith unto him, I am the way, the truth, and the life: no man cometh unto the Father, but by me"* (John 14:6, KJV).

Christ was sinless, yet He became our sin bearer. Instead of symbolically cleansing us from defilement and death, the Lord cleansed us from actual sin. It was through His sacrifice at Calvary that the Lord Jesus removed the ultimate obstacle, sin, that had caused centuries of estrangement between God and man, thereby allowing the restoration of intimate fellowship with the Father:

> For this is good and acceptable in the sight of God our Savior, who desires all men to be saved and to come to the knowledge of the truth. For there is one God and one Mediator between God and men, the Man Christ Jesus, who gave Himself a ransom for all, to be testified in due time. (1 Timothy 2:3-6)

HISTORY'S FOCUS

The Cross, central to all mankind, stands as God's ultimate revelation of supernatural love. Why?

More importantly, why did He go willingly to Calvary?

> *For when we were still without strength, in due time Christ died for the ungodly. For scarcely for a righteous man will one die; yet perhaps for a good man someone would even dare to die. But God demonstrates His own love toward us, in that while we were still sinners, Christ died for us. Much more then, having now been justified by His blood, we shall be saved from wrath through Him. For if when we were enemies we were reconciled to God through the death of His Son, much more, having been reconciled, we shall be saved by His life. And not only that, but we also rejoice in God through our Lord Jesus Christ, through whom we have now received the reconciliation.* (Romans 5:6:11)

Noted Bible teacher and author Andrew Murray wrote:

> There was no other way by which His love could redeem those whom He loved except by Him shedding His blood for them on the cross. It is because of this that He would not allow Himself to be turned aside by the terror of the cross, not even when it caused His soul to tremble and shudder. The cross tells us that He loved us so truly that His

love surmounted every difficulty—the curse of sin, and the hostility of man—and that His love has conquered and has won us for Himself. The cross is the triumphant symbol of eternal love. By the cross, love is seated on the throne, so that from the place of omnipotence it can now do for the beloved ones all that they desire.[3]

We were once bound in sin, but the Lamb of God, foretold throughout a number of centuries in the thirty-nine books of the Old Testament, delivered us. Through Him and the price He paid to set us free, we have salvation and redemption: *"In Him we have redemption through His blood, the forgiveness of sins, according to the riches of His grace"* (Ephesians 1:7). This redemption is what the apostle Paul referred to when he wrote: *"For you were bought at a price; therefore glorify God in your body and in your spirit, which are God's"* (1 Corinthians 6:20).

The death of Jesus on the cross was a deliberate murder, no accident. The Son of Man's blood was not spilled but was shed. Christ, who could have called all of heaven's angels to wage war on the Roman soldiers, instead went to Calvary voluntarily. He chose to die as a substitute for you and me. He shed His precious blood for us. Jesus told us candidly: *"Just as the Son of Man did not come to be served, but to serve, and to give His life a ransom for many"* (Matthew 20:28).

NEW COVENANT

Please note the major difference between atonement in the Old Testament and New Testament. I have mentioned this before, but it bears repeating. The late Derek Prince explained this difference in his book *Atonement*:

> In Hebrew the word [for atonement] is *kippur* and means "covering." The Day of Atonement was a day of *covering*. By the sacrifices offered on that day, the sins of the people were *covered*—but only for one year. The next year at the same time, their sins had to be covered once more. The sacrifices offered that day provided no permanent solution, therefore, to the problem of sin; they merely provided a temporary covering. On each successive Day of Atonement, that covering was extended for one more year.
>
> The picture of atonement in the New Testament is totally different. We see this when we contrast two passages in Hebrews—the book that deals, above all others, with Jesus as our High Priest and with the sacrifice He made on our behalf. [4]

By contrast, the blood sacrifice of Jesus Christ didn't just remind God's children of the problem of sin. His shed blood took away that problem, once and for all:

> *But Christ came as High Priest of the good things to come, with the greater and more perfect tabernacle not made with hands, that is, not of this creation. Not with the blood of goats and calves, but with His own blood He entered the*

Most Holy Place once for all, having obtained eternal redemption. For if the blood of bulls and goats and the ashes of a heifer, sprinkling the unclean, sanctifies for the purifying of the flesh, how much more shall the blood of Christ, who through the eternal Spirit offered Himself without spot to God, cleanse your conscience from dead works to serve the living God? And for this reason He is the Mediator of the new covenant, by means of death, for the redemption of the transgressions under the first covenant, that those who are called may receive the promise of the eternal inheritance. (Hebrews 9:11-15)

We know that *"without shedding of blood there is no remission"* (verse 22), therefore Jesus Christ offered Himself as the ultimate atonement sacrifice:

For Christ has not entered the holy places made with hands, which are copies of the true, but into heaven itself, now to appear in the presence of God for us; not that He should offer Himself often, as the high priest enters the Most Holy Place every year with blood of another—He then would have had to suffer often since the foundation of the world; but now, once at the end of the ages, He has appeared to put away sin by the sacrifice of Himself. And as it is appointed for men to die once, but after this the judgment, so Christ was offered once to bear the sins of many. (Hebrews 9:24-28)

Our precious Savior went to the cross to take our place, to atone for our sins, once and for all. Atonement is yours, for God has provided a new covenant. Because you have been atoned through the blood of Jesus Christ, you have moved into a new covenant, a covenant filled with many blessings. I have discussed seven of these, directly from Joel 2, throughout the book.

Because you have been atoned, you are redeemed. You have passed from death unto life. You have been reconciled to God. You are clean before Him and can ask for cleansing continually. You are sanctified, or set apart, for the Master's use. You are perfected. Best of all, you can come boldly before God's throne to enter His holy presence.

Always remember every promise of the Atonement throughout the Bible belongs to you. God is faithful. You can claim every blessing. You can walk into the presence of God today because you are bought with the blood of the Lamb.

ATONEMENT

You have been atoned, once and for all. The seven blessings of the Atonement—a double portion, financial abundance, restoration, miracles, God's divine presence, blessings upon your family, and deliverance—are yours for the claiming. Whatever God promised to His covenant people in the Old Testament holds true for New Testament believers, those covered by the "better covenant" spoken about throughout the book of Hebrews:

> *Now this is the main point of the things we are saying: We*
> *have such a High Priest, who is seated at the right hand of*

the throne of the Majesty in the heavens, a Minister of the sanctuary and of the true tabernacle which the Lord erected, and not man.

For every high priest is appointed to offer both gifts and sacrifices. Therefore it is necessary that this One also have something to offer. For if He were on earth, He would not be a priest, since there are priests who offer the gifts according to the law; who serve the copy and shadow of the heavenly things, as Moses was divinely instructed when he was about to make the tabernacle. For He said, "See that you make all things according to the pattern shown you on the mountain." But now He has obtained a more excellent ministry, inasmuch as He is also Mediator of a better covenant, which was established on better promises.

For if that first covenant had been faultless, then no place would have been sought for a second. (Hebrews 8:1-7)

You are on the greatest adventure you can ever imagine. The blood of the Lamb has been applied to your life. You have been atoned. You now have a personal relationship with God, a relationship that is eternal and unlike anything you have ever known. As your relationship grows from day to day and as you get to know Him better, you will come to love Him more and more.

You are under a better covenant, yet you have the blessings available from the Old Covenant, as well! Now, more than ever, you can unleash your Atonement blessings!

Are you ready?

12

UNLEASHING YOUR
DAY OF ATONEMENT BLESSINGS

And the LORD spoke to Moses, saying, "Speak to the children of Israel, and say to them: 'The feasts of the LORD, which you shall proclaim to be holy convocations, these are My feasts.... Also the tenth day of this seventh month shall be the Day of Atonement. It shall be a holy convocation for you; you shall afflict your souls, and offer an offering made by fire to the LORD."

—LEVITICUS 23:1-2, 27

These seven blessings of the Atonement are specific and astounding, which is why I spent an entire chapter on each one:

- A Double Portion
- Financial Abundance
- Restoration
- Miracles
- God's Divine Presence
- Blessings upon Your Family
- Deliverance

We know that God established the Day of Atonement, the most sacred day of the Jewish year, as an appointed (holy) time each year throughout both the Old and the New Testaments, and to be kept forever.

However, for nearly seventeen centuries, these powerful truths have been mostly ignored and even rejected by Christians. Thankfully, that is now changing. It must change! There is too much at stake during these crucial, prophetic days.

Let me urge you unleash your blessings in three very practical ways: your life, your finances, and your greatest purpose in today's world!

Unleash God's Plan of Atonement in Your Life

In my *Seven Blessings of the Passover* book, I used an illustration that fits here perfectly:

> At almost every county fair, carnival, and fun park, you see children and their parents on carousels. It seems that everyone loves to ride the festively painted horses, swans, and other figurines. Have you noticed, though, that there comes a time when boys and girls start realizing that going around in circles is baby stuff? Suddenly, at a certain age, the young people want to do other things at the carnival that are more challenging.
>
> I've often wondered why so many believers in the Lamb of God are content to ride throughout life on spiritual carousels. Too often we fall at the foot of the Cross and

accept Jesus Christ as Savior, then we look around, see an apparently happy group going around in circles, figure God must be in the center of it, and ride along. Sadly, it gets easier and easier to just go around in circles, never really understanding that the path from the cross of Calvary to God's throne room in heaven is often a rugged road. [1]

How do you stop going around in circles? How do you get started on that rugged road that leads to fulfillment, purpose, and eternal rewards? Begin by embracing the cross, where your atonement was made:

> *Then Jesus said to His disciples, "If anyone desires to come after Me, let him deny himself, and take up his cross, and follow Me. For whoever desires to save his life will lose it, but whoever loses his life for My sake will find it. For what profit is it to a man if he gains the whole world, and loses his own soul? Or what will a man give in exchange for his soul? For the Son of Man will come in the glory of His Father with His angels, and then He will reward each according to his works.* (Matthew 16:24-27)

What was Jesus telling us to do? He's saying to die to self. The apostle Paul wrote often of this need:

> *What shall we say then? Shall we continue in sin that grace may abound? Certainly not! How shall we who died to sin*

live any longer in it? Or do you not know that as many of us as were baptized into Christ Jesus were baptized into His death? Therefore we were buried with Him through baptism into death, that just as Christ was raised from the dead by the glory of the Father, even so we also should walk in newness of life. For if we have been united together in the likeness of His death, certainly we also shall be in the likeness of His resurrection, knowing this, that our old man was crucified with Him, that the body of sin might be done away with, that we should no longer be slaves of sin. For he who has died has been freed from sin. Now if we died with Christ, we believe that we shall also live with Him, knowing that Christ, having been raised from the dead, dies no more. Death no longer has dominion over Him. For the death that He died, He died to sin once for all; but the life that He lives, He lives to God. Likewise you also, reckon yourselves to be dead indeed to sin, but alive to God in Christ Jesus our Lord. (Romans 6:1-11)

How do you unleash your atoned, redeemed life by dying? It is simple, but not easy:

Most assuredly, I say to you, unless a grain of wheat falls into the ground and dies, it remains alone; but if it dies, it produces much grain. He who loves his life will lose it, and he who hates his life in this world will keep it for eternal life. If anyone serves Me, let him follow Me; and where I am,

*there My servant will be also. If anyone serves Me, him My
Father will honor.* (John 12:24-26)

Following Christ means unleashing Him to work in you
every day by embracing the cross, dying to self, and accepting the
changes that He brings.

Unleash God's Atonement Blessings in Your Finances

In addition to unleashing your life by dying to self, it is time for
you to unleash the financial blessings of the Atonement. I won't
belabor the points made earlier in chapter 5, but let me remind you
of Exodus 23:15, where the children of Israel were given instructions
for the feast seasons: *"None shall appear before Me empty."*

Granted, the children of Israel were required to bring more
than twenty different offerings to the Lord, both great and some
small. During the Atonement, however, the offering was unique
by promising the seven specific blessings that have been discussed
throughout this book.

Once they received the word, the children of Israel gave in
obedience, and God blessed them beyond measure. That should
settle it, once and for all!

Today, what is the best thing we have to give to the Lord? We
must give ourselves, which is why I started this chapter with dying to
self. Do not give your money to God if you have not given yourself.
You cannot buy a personal relationship with God. God can get along
without your money. It is for your benefit that God requires you to

give, but He has an order. He wants you first. Then, out of the giving yourself, the other blessings will follow.

Beyond yourself, your Atonement gift should be a special offering, not your tithe or a "regular" offering. It should be sacrificial. It should be generous. As I said in chapter 5, it should be radical if you want extreme results in your life as a result!

How much should it be? Only God can reveal that to you. Ask Him. I know from personal experience that He will give you the amount. Whatever it is should be worthy to commemorate what He has done for you through His shed blood.

God will multiply your special offering back in supernatural ways. God has a wonderful plan for your financial future. As I wrote many times in chapter 5, the Bible is chockfull of promises of the Father's blessings for those who understand and obey the Creator's fixed laws of sowing and reaping. As you apply His kingdom principles, you can live an abundant life that is filled with financial miracles!

What has God put into your hand? According to God's Word, He provides seed to the sower. The Word of God declares in 2 Corinthians 9:10, *"Now may He who supplies seed to the sower, and bread for food, supply and multiply the seed you have sown and increase the fruits of your righteousness."*

God also promises: *"Give, and it will be given to you: good measure, pressed down, shaken together, and running over will be put into your bosom. For with the same measure that you use, it will be measured back to you"* (Luke 6:38).

Give your special Atonement gift during the fall season, and see what God does in your life. From what I have seen and experienced, it will be the most fertile time of the year for your seed! What could be better than the former and latter rains happening together to bring a powerful, supernatural harvest?

Unleashing your finances during the Atonement season is directly related to obeying God's laws of giving, but His divine design for your financial success will not happen without your cooperation!

The release of God's blessings in your life is connected to your obedience, for the Bible declares: *"And all these blessings shall come upon you and overtake you, because you obey the voice of the LORD your God"* (Deuteronomy 28:2). God has a divine plan for your financial success! These timeless keys are revealed throughout the Bible, and they are given to help you implement God's plan and to help you succeed in everything you do!

UNLEASH YOUR GREATER PURPOSE

God does not give the seven blessings of the Atonement lightly. There is a purpose much larger than you or me. The reason for a supernatural outpouring of blessings related to the Atonement should always point to the Great Commission: *"Go therefore and make disciples of all the nations, baptizing them in the name of the Father and of the Son and of the Holy Spirit, teaching them to observe all things that I have commanded you; and lo, I am with you always, even to the end of the age"* (Matthew 28:19-20).

God is moving mightily today. He is shaking the nations. The message of God's great plan of Atonement is reaching hearts around the globe. We have a great work to do. He has promised to supply whatever we need to accomplish all that He has called us to do:

Most assuredly, I say to you, he who believes in Me, the works that I do he will do also; and greater works than these he will do, because I go to My Father. And whatever you ask in My name, that I will do, that the Father may be glorified in the Son. If you ask anything in My name, I will do it. (John 14:12-14)

Sowing always precedes reaping, and seedtime always precedes harvest. The Atonement seed you sow in faith will produce a harvest of abundance and blessings on your life and will take the Gospel message of Jesus Christ to the nations of the world.

May God bless you abundantly—through all seven blessings of the Atonement—during the coming days! I look forward to rejoicing with you in heaven for all that Jesus Christ accomplishes in you and through you as a result of the unleashed Atonement blessings in your life!

NOTES

Introduction

1. James Strong, *The Exhaustive Concordance of the Bible* (Peabody, MA: Hendrickson Publishers, n.d.), definition #5150.
2. Strong, *Exhaustive Concordance*, #2282.
3. Strong, *Exhaustive Concordance*, #2287.
4. For a more complete study on all of the feasts, especially the Passover, refer to my book, *Seven Blessings of the Passover* (Dallas: Clarion Call Marketing, Inc., 2005). Portions of this section are taken from that book.
5. Benny Hinn, *Lamb of God: Yesterday, Today & Forever* (Dallas: Clarion Call Marketing, Inc., 2004), 38. Used by permission.
6. Hinn, *Lamb of God*, 40.

Chapter 1

1. Yom Kippur, www.biblicalholidays.com.
2. Edward Chumley, *The Seven Festivals of the Messiah* (Shippensberg, PA: Destiny Image, 2001), 150–51.
3. Eugene H. Merrill, *An Historical Survey of the Old Testament* (Nutley, NJ: Craig Press, 1966), 146.

Chapter 2

1. Richard Booker, *Jesus in the Feasts of Israel* (Shippensburg, PA: Destiny Image Publishers, 1987), 91.

Chapter 3

1. "Dog Days," www.britannica.com.
2. "Dog Days," http://encarta.msn.com.
3. NAAF Project, www.neveragain.org.
4. Jewish Virtual Library, www.jewishvirtuallibrary.org.

Chapter 6

1. I am just hitting the highlights of this powerful story, but I encourage you to read the entire account in Benny Hinn's amazing book, *Total Recovery* (Irving, TX: Clarion Call Marketing, 2005).
2. Charles Haddon Spurgeon, "Peter's Restoration," sermon delivered on July 22, 1888, at the Metropolitan Tabernacle, Newington, London.
3. Charles Haddon Spurgeon, "Truth Stranger Than Fiction," sermon delivered on May 30, 1886, at the Metropolitan Tabernacle in Newington, London.

Chapter 8

1. A.W. Tozer, *The Divine Conquest* (Camp Hill, PA: Christian Publications, 1950, 1978), 43.
2. Smith Wigglesworth, *Smith Wigglesworth on Faith* (New Kensington, PA: Whitaker House, 1998), 175.

Chapter 9

1. Charles Haddon Spurgeon, "Household Salvation," sermon preached November 5, 1871.

Chapter 11

1. Billy Graham, *Peace With God* (Nashville: Word Publishing, 1984), 35.
2. Maxwell Whyte, *The Power of the Blood* (Springdale, PA: Whitaker House, 1973), 21–22.
3. Andrew Murray, *The Blood of the Cross* (Fort Washington, PA: Christian Literature Crusade, 1995), 77–78.
4. Derek Prince, *Atonement: Your Appointment with God* (Grand Rapids, MI: Chosen Books, 2000), 11–12.

Chapter 12

1. Steve Munsey, *Seven Blessings of the Passover* (Dallas: Clarion Call Marketing, 2005), 119.